D1525323

Winning the War
Against Youth Gangs

Winning the War Against Youth Gangs

A Guide for Teens, Families, and Communities

VALERIE WIENER

GREENWOOD PRESS
Westport, Connecticut • London

Library of Congress Cataloging-in-Publication Data

Wiener, Valerie.
   Winning the war against youth gangs : a guide for teens, families,
and communities / Valerie Wiener.
      p.   cm.
   Includes bibliographical references and index.
   ISBN 0–313–30819–5 (alk. paper)
   1. Gangs—United States—Handbooks, manuals, etc.   2. Gang
prevention—United States—Handbooks, manuals, etc.   3. Gang members—
United States—Rehabilitation.   4. Juvenile delinquency—United
States—Prevention.   I. Title.
HV6439.U5W53   1999
364.1'06'608350973—dc21   99–22097

British Library Cataloguing in Publication Data is available.

Library of Congress Catalog Card Number: 99–22097
ISBN: 0–313–30819–5

First published in 1999

Greenwood Press, 88 Post Road West, Westport, CT 06881
An imprint of Greenwood Publishing Group, Inc.
www.greenwood.com

Printed in the United States of America

The paper used in this book complies with the
Permanent Paper Standard issued by the National
Information Standards Organization (Z39.48–1984).

10 9 8 7 6 5 4 3 2 1

Years ago, I realized that I would probably never be a parent. Knowing and accepting this was okay, though, because I also knew that you do not have to be a parent to care about children who hunger for your love. So, to those wonderful children—of all ages—who need a listener, a friend, a hug . . . I dedicate this book with all the love I have to give.

Contents

Preface

One of the greatest adventures for an author involves the growth of ideas from one book to the next. My experiences in writing for youths and their families are not unlike those of many other authors who write about a particular subject area.

In 1995, I wrote my first book about youth and family issues, *Gang Free: Friendship Choices for Today's Youth*. The book deals with how teenagers build their first friendships of choice, how they pick the groups they join, and how they resolve their basic social needs during adolescence. It is a comprehensive look at the issues of adolescence from the perspective of teens and their families. Because of *Gang Free*, I moved to the issue of gangs and continue to work with media and community organizations throughout the United States and Canada to help resolve gang-related issues.

In 1997, while I was serving my first session as a Nevada state senator, Greenwood Publishing Group approached me to write a book for school and public libraries. They asked for a book that would focus on how to keep youths from joining gangs and how to help disengage those who had already joined. I agreed. After I completed my legislative session, I immersed myself in this book project, and *Winning the War Against Youth Gangs: A Guide for Teens, Families, and Communities* took seed.

I read several dozen books on the youth gang issue and conducted original research with youths in nine states, representing every region and type of neighborhood in the country. Young people—270 of them—who come from both healthy and unhealthy family and community environments participated. To secure information from them in the most candid way, I assured survey participants that they would not be identifiable from their quotes. This is why I identify them only by first name, age, and the type of community in which they live (such as urban).

My references to youths throughout this book are often interchanged with such descriptors as young people, children, young adults, emerging adults, adolescents, and teenagers. Often my word choice indicates something very specific to that age. In other places, I interchange the references, because the point I might be making is universal to children—across age lines—who might be involved with, or affected by, the particular issue.

I designed *Winning the War Against Youth Gangs* to address the youth gang issue in understandable, manageable terms. This is why I organized the book into four parts. Part I, "Resolving Basic Needs," describes many basic issues and needs that all children have in common. Part II, "The Gang Life," addresses how and why certain children enter—and sometimes exit— gang alliances. Part III, "Winning the War Through Collaboration," focuses on how several integral components of the child's life and community can work together to resolve youths' involvement with gangs. Part IV, "Family and Child," analyzes the critical influence of families—and the children themselves—as these youths approach important life choices. These include whether to join a youth gang or whether to leave a gang to which they are already connected.

Throughout the book, I have integrated statistics and quotes from the kids themselves to illustrate the real-world impact of youth gangs on the lives of our nation's children. I have done this to allow the young people to communicate directly with each reader at a more personal level.

Ultimately, *Winning the War Against Youth Gangs* underscores that the influence of youth gangs is not distinctive only to inner cities and minorities. Young people are struggling with these peer-alliance issues and demands in communities—of all sizes and locations—across the country. To resolve these pressures, members of each community need to work together collaboratively to provide young people with positive, realistic choices for their lives. Only in this way can we, as individuals and communities, hope to influence the growth and impact of youth gang activities in our country.

Acknowledgments

Thank you. Thank you. Thank you.

To the many, many people who have contributed to this book, I give my appreciation and gratitude for the unselfish expertise and insight they shared with me. From the whisper of an idea to the writing of the dedication, dozens of people have helped me deliver this book in its final form.

When I first decided to write a book about youth gangs, I wanted to approach it like no other author had done. I felt almost driven to let the kids themselves speak through me as much as possible. For example, I have served for several years as a judge for the Inner City Games writing competition in Las Vegas, Nevada. These writing entries—hundreds of them each year—consistently demonstrate the innermost thoughts and feelings of today's children. I decided to put some of this great talent to work in *Winning the War Against Youth Gangs*. With the help and support of Las Vegas gaming executive and community activist Elaine Wynn and her able Inner City Games staff assistant, Joyce Walker, I was able to secure the insightful creative writings of fifteen talented youths. Excerpts from the following writers begin each chapter: Angela, 10, urban; Cremson, 15, suburban; Gwendolyn, 13, suburban; Jennifer, 18, urban; John, 13, suburban; Kimberly, 18, urban; Leslie, 13, suburban; Lily, 13, inner city; Mark, 14, suburban; Neil, 17, inner city; Renee, 14, urban; Starla, 17, inner city; Stephanie, 18, suburban; T.S., 15, urban; and Will, 17, inner city.

Working persistently with me from the very beginning of the survey stage was Al Crosby. A friend since eighth grade, he now serves as director of detention for the Family and Youth Service Department of Clark County,

Nevada. Al opened the doors for me to contact other detention and youth-service directors across the country. They then helped me contact youths in detention centers, youth programs, and other community organizations to participate in extensive field survey work. For their irreplaceable assistance, I want to thank the following youth-service professionals: Barbara Dooley, Tennessee; Ron Fryer, Florida; Mary Furnas, Nebraska; Vel Garner, Colorado; Wayne Liddle, Michigan; Anne Nelson, Utah; George Pippin, Jr., Delaware; and Larry Springer, California. Youths from nine states contributed to the writing of this book with their statistical input and candid quotations. To all 270 youths, I offer a great big thanks for enriching the substance and heart of this book.

In addition, I want to thank Edward M. Bernstein and Susan Boswell, who so aptly represent the ideals of their organization, the National Conference for Community and Justice (Las Vegas), and who allowed me to work with the 1998 youth participants at Camp Anytown. I am also pleased that, thanks to my friend Doug Carson, I was able to tap insights from youth leaders who attended Nevada's 1998 Hugh O'Brian Youth Foundation summer leadership program. Ditto for Mary Ellen Heise and the fine input from Leadership Las Vegas Youth.

To my patient, supportive, ever-responsive editor, Emily Birch, I want to give a very special pat on the back. Emily encouraged me at every stage of this book's development. I consider her an outstanding leader and teammate and look forward to working with her again on books involving our nation's children.

Though last in the acknowledgments, but always first in my thoughts . . . an ever-growing appreciation to my friends and family who give me hugs when I need them and remind me often to laugh . . . just for the health of it!

Part I

Resolving Basic Needs

Chapter 1

It All Begins with Self

Sitting on my porch, "Who am I?" I wonder.
Two scoops of sugar in my tea I stir.
Secretly guarding my heart, I build a fortress made of lumber,
Preparing for the obstacles that might occur.

So unsure of my very being,
So insecure of my very right to life,
Looking is not seeing.
And living is so much more than playing mother and wife.

Jennifer, 18, Urban

THE SHADOW GENERATION

Welcome to the world of the *shadow generation*—those people in our population, especially our youth, who are searching to answer the question "Who am I?" and how this impacts everything else they think and do. The shadow generation is not necessarily defined by age. Rather, it includes all those people who are trying to establish distinctive identities, purposes, and directions. They are striving to create their own positive relationships with others as well. For the purposes of our journey in this book, however, we will focus our attention on youths, particularly on teenagers.

Our children, especially our teenagers, live in a crowded stage of life. Once they make their way beyond adolescence, they are expected to have all the answers. Until that time, they struggle to find out who they are and what they should expect of themselves and others, those who are close and not so close to them. They constantly try to figure out the whats, whys, and hows in their lives.

One of the greatest ways to learn involves observation—watching how other people act and react. Young people "shadow" others to model themselves after people they admire. For most youths, these early role models are their parents or caregivers. From infancy, children create their self-images based, in large part, on how these adults handle and care for them.

As they grow older, teenagers broaden their people watching. At the same time teenagers are peering outward at others, they are also looking inward at themselves. Consciously or subconsciously, they weigh whether others' thoughts, attitudes, actions, and reactions will work for them.

It is normal for children to develop in this way. They are not weird or weak because they are not yet sure of what to say or do in certain situations. This learning process is much more sophisticated. It includes observation, understanding, evaluation, and response.

SO WHO AM I?

How do young people initially define themselves? By how tall they are, the color of their hair, the size clothing they wear? Teenagers, in particular, demonstrate great sensitivity about their "looks." They care about their appearance and its impact on how people respond to them.

Mira Kirshanbaum, in her book *Parent/Teen Breakthrough* (1991), responds to the universal teen question "Who am I?" by listing some of the ways teenagers create reference points for their identities. A sample of this list includes style of dress, religion, politics, music preferences, sexual orientation, where the teen lives, the teen's level of ambition, and what the teen likes to do for fun.

Two additional interrelated criteria help define teenagers and the identities they seek. These are the people they choose as friends and the groups they join for companionship.

As adolescents pursue answers to the "Who am I?" question, one message will be clear. Whatever criteria teenagers prefer to create a personal identity, they will achieve a distinctive identity, with many components. Parents need to remember that this process is a normal one for adolescents. The search for self serves an integral purpose in the definition of adolescence.

"It starts with the family." *(John, 16, Rural)*

"Oddly, I don't have such a positive self-image. I am outgoing in selecting friends and the things that I do, but I don't think I value myself enough. I don't really like me, but I never portray that part of me to my friends." *(Xochitl, 20, Inner City)*

"I'm a very determined and outgoing person. There are times when I don't feel very good about myself and my appearance, but that's a natural part of growing up. You need to have a confident view of yourself to make honest friends." *(Amber, 14, Urban)*

Teenagers sometimes start their journey into self-identity by determining who they are *not*. Often this manifests in their not wanting to be anything like their parents, which is normal.

SELF-ESTEEM

Teenagers probably think that the whole world knows what is going on in their heads, no matter what they do to protect themselves. The more they try to display confidence in what they do, the more they stumble at the most inappropriate times.

Vulnerability

Young adulthood prompts feelings of vulnerability about self-confidence. Part of this discomfort comes from confusion. Youths often demonstrate "different selves" at different times, and with different people. Sometimes teenagers keep parts of themselves, and how they think, private from their best friends. Yet they might be eager to share these same important messages with someone else, even a stranger.

Inner confusion runs rampant in adolescents. Sensitivities reign. Teenagers especially tend to be secretive because of fear, often the fear of ridicule. They can also be irritable because they intensely dislike interference from other people who cannot really understand them. This is a period in their lives when the need for private time and space is extraordinarily important. Rules versus self-rule.

"I don't like it when my parents tell me to stay home when they never listened to rules." *(Jessie, 14, Inner City)*

"This is almost an essential part of my everyday life. Respecting the rules laid down not only by my parents but everyone else is very important to me. Coming from England, with English grandparents living with me, respecting authority is also very important." *(Reza, 16, Urban)*

Learning how to balance outside rules and self-rule helps teenagers take control of and responsibility for their lives and develop a healthy *self-esteem.* What is self-esteem, anyway? Dr. Nathaniel Branden, an early pioneer of the self-esteem movement, describes the concept in his book *The Power of Self-Esteem* (1992). He defines self-esteem as:

The experience that we are appropriate to life and to the requirements of life. More specifically, self-esteem is *confidence* in our ability to think and to cope with the basic challenges of life. Self-esteem is confidence in our right to be happy, the feeling of being worthy, deserving, entitled to assert our needs and wants, and to enjoy the fruits of our efforts.

Empowerment

Obviously, self-esteem means more than an inherent sense of self-worth. It includes powerful human need, essential to youths and their becoming who they are, as well as influencing who they want to become. *Empowerment.*

When young people have real confidence in themselves, and in what they think and do, they are empowered. By continuing to be aware of this and other qualities in themselves, teenagers can find the energy and motivation to face challenges, complete tasks, and respond positively to relationships. They can enjoy satisfaction from what they think, say, and do. They thrive.

"I have never joined a youth gang, because I am happy just the way I am. I have a great family life and many friends. I am my own person and do not choose to associate with that group of people." *(Jodi, 17, Urban)*

"I feel really good about myself. I don't have any hang-ups about life or about myself." *(Amy, 15, Suburban)*

"I am fortunate enough to have a loving family. They have in-
stilled in me good morals and a positive nature to resist the urge
to join a youth gang." *(Marianne, 17, Urban)*

No one—not even a teenager—is bestowed with self-esteem. We all need
to develop it. Self-esteem is not static. Anyone can challenge it at any time,
any place. In fact, the more choices and the more decisions a person needs
to make—whether to do drugs, break the law, call home about being late,
not driving while drinking—the more crucial will be the need for self-
esteem.

A child's heritage, racial background, or family achievements cannot define self-esteem. No one can rely on these cosmetic considerations to define
who they are or are not. To work for them, self-esteem must come from
within each person. This means that positive feelings about who teenagers
are, what they think, and how they live their lives must originate in their
own positive thoughts of themselves. It is never too early for a child to
groom high self-esteem. It can start with simple thoughts and actions. For
example, when young children realize that they have choices about who
they call friend, they are developing a strong sense of self. When they know
they do not have to wait for someone else to pick them first, these children—and teenagers—recognize their own personal value and the right to
grow healthy relationships in their lives.

"I am strong, good, and quick-witted. I am okay with who I am
as an individual. This is important for self-identity." *(Mary, 16,
Suburban)*

As youths grow and nurture their self-esteem, their choices will expand.
They will demonstrate willingness, and probably eagerness, to venture beyond their own *safety zone*—their own place of personal comfort—and try
new things, in new ways, with new people. As young adults experiment,
they will often fall short of perfection, or even success, as defined by others.
However, teenagers' willingness to venture beyond "the known" produces
success in itself.

"Having friends helps you get to know other people and realize
what kinds of people are out there." *(Charla, 15, Suburban)*

"Picking my circle of friends is very important. I know I should
be careful not to narrow myself. In order to make it in this coun-

try we need to work with people from all groups, colors, and races." *(Mayte, 19, Urban)*

"I think it is important to share time and interests with others so they can get to know you well." *(Jason, 17, Inner City)*

Self-Respect

Young people cannot define *self-respect* by what and how others think about them. So they need to be careful not to fall prey to becoming "approval-seekers." They should not let how others behave toward them solely define how they think about themselves.

A healthy sense of self-respect helps young adults demonstrate how they feel about themselves in relation to other people in many ways. Body language—posture, mannerisms, gestures, expressions—projects a strong dose of self-appreciation. Forthrightness and honesty help position youths positively with themselves and others. How young people give and receive compliments, as well as criticism, reflects self-respect. A willingness to be curious, open-minded, and adventurous enhances self-respect. A good sense of humor, assertiveness, flexibility, and good judgment are also powerful "self" builders. These, plus honest self-awareness and well-earned self-pride, help young people realize that they do not need to make themselves appear superior to others to elevate themselves.

Certainly, parents and other caregivers should assume an important role in helping teenagers in their pursuit of self-respect. All adults who come into or influence teens have the potential to affect what and how these young adults think about themselves. Adults serve as role models for those who watch them in hopes of learning about themselves and their world. Therefore, adults need to realize that every action they take can have an impact on how an observant teenager will act and react to situations. Knowing this, adults, especially parents and other caregivers, should accept the challenge and take advantage of the opportunity to help shape the thoughts and behaviors of children and teenagers.

At the same time, teenagers should also take responsibility by selecting their role models carefully. These role models will necessarily include adults. However, each youth's friends and other peers also serve as role models. Teenagers have the right to be particular in who and how they choose the people they want to emulate. This decision is a crucial one, because it will ultimately affect how youths define themselves.

"I have accomplished a lot and have high self-respect. I think my friends should feel the same way about themselves so we can share in our successes and cultures." *(Neil, 17, Suburban)*

Self-Acceptance

Self-acceptance also contributes to self-esteem. This does not mandate young people to remain ever-constant and stay the way they are right now. It means that they are empowered to experiment. They can make changes in their lives, and they can have confidence in themselves for having said or done something new. For example, a teenager might express an original idea in English class, without worrying about what other classmates might think. Or, a teen can go to a history museum, without wondering how friends might react. Or . . . refuse to participate in a group activity, or respond to a demand, without questioning the right to say "no."

The ability to make personal choices often requires courage. It takes strength to consider options, especially when more than one choice looks good to the youth. One key to suitable decision making is practice. Each decision that produces a feel-good, appropriate, legal result reinforces within the youth the ability to make that kind of decision again, and again. This does not mean that courage is easy. However, in the long run, it is ultimately easier for emerging adults to make the right choice than to have to live indefinitely with the wrong one.

With enhanced empowerment, teenagers can become responsible for all aspects of their lives. These aspects include their goals, actions, ideals, decisions, personal happiness, and relationships. Self-esteem and empowerment do not come easily, and often the struggle to develop them can be an overwhelming task for a teenager. Defeat—or the perception of defeat—can discourage an emerging adult from attempting empowerment. Personal success, however modest, will lead to the next and . . . the next!

In the real world, self-acceptance helps children of all ages trust themselves and their own decisions. They can face challenges realistically. They also recognize that they can and do make a difference with their thoughts, actions, and reactions. Self-acceptance will encourage lifelong learning, as well as teaching. Young people with high self-acceptance can express their autonomy, while appreciating the value of other people in their lives.

"I feel that I am in a comfortable position with myself and others. I am usually content and secure with myself." *(Jonathan, 17, Suburban)*

"I am fairly happy with who I am. I think high self-esteem does affect a person's outlook on friendship. When you care about—and accept—yourself, you tend to care about the type of friends you choose." *(Alyssa, 15, Suburban)*

"JET TRACKING"

Even when teenagers have generally high self-esteem, they will have experiences that prompt questionable feelings about themselves. This can happen when they are sick, tired, or overloaded, or when they are living through important changes. Questions might arise, such as: "What's wrong with me?" or "Why do things like this always happen to me?" or "I'm not strong enough or smart enough to handle this problem."

Young people need to appreciate their capabilities. Equally important, they should not shortchange themselves when faced with a challenge. In moments of vulnerability, parents and other influential adults must encourage adolescents not to quit on themselves.

Adults can start helping youths by listening to them more often. This means listening to them without prejudice or predetermined thinking. It also involves recognizing the value in how these emerging adults think and express themselves. Related to this, adults should teach and demonstrate to youths the value of commitment to their ideas, and, at the same time, the necessity for flexibility. They should point out how rarely situations in life can be approached from only one perspective or point of view, and that it is okay to ask questions. Another important message for adults to impart to teens involves risk taking. They should encourage these emerging adults to break out of their safety zones to make mistakes. They need to help youths understand it is okay to experiment with their lives, as long as the chosen activities do not break the law, hurt others or themselves, or negatively impact their own long-term health and welfare.

Emerging adults endeavor to understand if their ideas and actions will ever be noticed or respected or, hope upon hope, make a difference. Each day, every day, our teens struggle to learn as much as they can, so that they can take the next step into the adult world. They also face additional pressures from the outside that compound the growing-up process. This layering of pressure upon pressure puts them on the *jet track* to adulthood. I discuss this rush to adulthood in my book *Gang Free* (1995).

It would be easy to fall back on the reasons this jet track has been forged. Some sociologists put the responsibility on dysfunctional or overloaded families. Others point to the media—with their ability to extend our senses and, ultimately, our experiences beyond the here and the now. Many trumpet the computer age and a high-stress world, with its nanosecond clock that sweeps us away unknowingly. If given multiple-choice alternatives, "all of the above" would be the right answer.

We need to realize, however, that these multiple sources of fast-paced living—and ultimate expectations of our children—have resulted in our accepting as "normal" the rushing process of our children. We are pushing them out of childhood into adulthood, without a momentary stop in "teen-hood."

At the other end of the spectrum, too many young people experience the *involvement void*—growing up with little or no parental involvement or concern. These children and young adults do not have markers, because their parents invest little time or energy in their children's growing up. They set few, if any, standards for their children, and they have minimal expectations of, and commitments to, their offspring.

Some parents ignore the teen years by stereotyping their children. This helps them avoid becoming intimate with their adolescents as individuals. Others sweep children past adolescence, because it is easier to deal with adults than with teens. Still others hurry their teens along, because they seek their companionship as equals and confidants. And today, many, too many, abandon their children to let others—often not the best choices—raise their children in haphazard ways. Or, they let the children themselves struggle for survival without any adult involvement or commitment.

Whatever the reasons, we sweep our children into adulthood. At both extremes, we package these children as grown-ups, or we force them into adulthood through abandonment or neglect. When adults confuse, ignore, fail to support, or stymie young people, these children turn elsewhere for support. Their friends, who would play an important part in their development anyway, take on an even more important role. Just like them, their friends are also zooming through life on the jet track.

Chapter Highlights

- Today's young people qualify as the *shadow generation*: they spend a great deal of time and energy following others.
- The earliest lessons for children come from observing how their parents and other caregivers behave.
- Self-exploration constitutes the first step that youths initiate in learning who they are, what they think, and how they want to live their lives.

- *Self-esteem* means more than an inherent sense of self-worth. It defines a child's confidence in his or her ability to think, to cope, to be happy, to feel worthy, to be entitled to assert personal needs and wants, and to enjoy the fruits of individual efforts.

- Self-esteem is something youths develop. No one gives it to them. They are not born with it, and it does not just happen.

- With self-esteem, teenagers can stretch beyond their *safety zones* to expand their choices for thoughts, actions, and reactions.

- Self-esteem provides a foundation for young people to trust in, and accept, themselves and others.

- Adolescents normally crave independence to experiment with their own choices in matters that affect their lives.

- Even when they generally have high self-esteem, teenagers will experience times when they do not feel good about themselves.

- Programming our children for the *jet track*, society expects them to be super-performers in everything they attempt, from school to home responsibilities to social activities.

- The jet track results from a combination of factors, including modern family dynamics, the media, economics, and high-tech living.

- "Jet tracking" means that we accept as "normal" the rushing process that pushes our children from early childhood into adulthood, with little or no time to treat the teen years as a distinct process.

- Some parents, however, set few if any, standards for their children. They have minimal expectations of, and commitments to, their children. This results in the *involvement void*, which stifles adolescent development. Other parents abandon their children, which requires these youth to rush into adulthood for survival.

Chapter 2

Peer Impact:
The Group Influence

I see my friends go down the wrong pathway.
The mistakes that they make have a price they must pay.
I choose a different course for my life.
I don't want to cause my family too much strife.

I stay away from drugs.
. . . Don't hang around with the thugs.
People these days are so confused.
They do anything they want to keep themselves amused.

My parents can be good examples.
But they're not always there when I'm asked to sample.
You've got to take it upon yourself to do what's right.
Resisting the temptation is always a fight.

There are pressures you face everywhere.
But all you need to do is find friends who care.

Starla, 17, Inner City

What does it take to do what is right?
What does it take to follow the light?
What does it take to stand for your beliefs?
I know when it's over there is so much relief.

What does it take to go against your peers?
I know in this life there are so many fears.

I sit in my room and think out loud.
How would it be not to follow the crowd?

Standing up tall, remembering where they are from . . .
Proud to be who they are and what they've become.
This is something very powerful and true.
I just wish you only knew.

It's not in the sky or in the sand.
But knowing who you are and where you stand.

Stephanie, 18, Suburban

FROM PARENTS . . . TO FRIENDS

During the search for who they are, teenagers struggle with a *dual identity*. They are still children—or considered so—in their own homes. Yet society expects these same "children" to use this time in their lives to learn how to be adults. For the first time in the lives of most teenagers—or, in too many situations, for those in their preteens—the idea of "being two people" occurs. They coexist as one person with two identities: the child and the emerging adult.

This emerging experience can produce great fear in the youth. This fear involves the teen's uncertainty about revealing an inner self to friends. Yet this revelation to friends provides the very expression that helps teenagers remove their own uncertainties. This translates into "being real" with friends in ways they might not be able to demonstrate to their own parents.

> "A friend is someone you can go to for comfort, someone you can tell anything, someone who understands you like no one else." *(Laquitta, 17, Urban)*

> ". . . someone who doesn't just agree with me. It's a person who can tell me when I'm wrong." *(Jackie, 16, Urban)*

> "A friend always supports you, while pushing for your best interests, and cares no matter what you may do." *(Lynn, 20, Rural)*

> "Friendship is the supporting force that enables me to survive the trying times through the various stages of my growth." *(Frank, 17, Suburban)*

"Friendship doesn't replace my family, but it does give me an extra boost of happiness." *(Heather, 15, Rural)*

Early friendship means taking risks. Teens risk the vulnerability of exposing themselves, and all their imperfections, to another person, often a stranger. However, the miracle of friendship surfaces when adolescents realize that their friends are experiencing parallel fears and insecurities. Friendship translates into a trust that says: "I care enough about you to be here for you, even when I might disagree with you, even when you are not your best."

Knowing the importance of friendship in their personal growth and development will help ease teenagers through difficult times. Friendship can serve as a challenging, rewarding, and supportive force in their lives.

EARLY FRIENDSHIP EXPERIENCES

Friendship fluctuates. It draws its very definition and life from the ever-changing emotions and activities of its participants. Friendship is never completely equal nor reciprocal.

Typical Friendships

No typical friendship exists. Each teenager has the capability to form friendships that have distinctive shapes and forms, through the people who define and give life to them. However, friendships do contain certain qualities that help inspire their continuity. Nearly ninety percent of the 270 youths who participated in the research for this book indicated *trust* as the most important factor in a growing friendship. Also important to friendship development are honesty, loyalty, commitment, and mutual respect. In addition, many respondents described a friend as someone who "is there for you."

Total communication helps teenagers make connections with others. This involves their speaking ability—getting their messages across to others in the ways they intend. It also involves their listening skills—hearing, processing, understanding, and responding to the messages of others. Once teenagers master total communication, their ability to associate with others, including peers and adults, is enhanced. Total communication helps teenagers answer several basic needs. These fundamental psychological requirements, according to Dr. Don Dinkmeyer in his book *Raising a Responsible Child* (1973), are the needs to:

- Be loved and accepted.
- Be secure and relatively free of threat.
- Belong, to identify themselves as part of a group.
- Be approved and recognized.
- Move toward independence, responsibility, and decision making.

While doing research for my book *Gang Free* (1995), I discovered other needs. These include teenagers' needs to:

- Distinguish their own individuality.
- Share time, space, and interests with others.
- Develop definitions and applications for reward, punishment, success, and failure.
- Recognize the potential to make a difference.
- For some, establish and exert power over others.

Peer Shock

When teenagers reach out beyond their home life to form their first extended friendships, they place themselves in positions of uncertainty. Early in the friendship process, teenagers offer and accept limited assurances and guarantees. This does not mean that teenagers intentionally avoid the qualities of friendship. Rather, they just do not know what friendship expects and demands.

Friendship offers teenagers exposure to new ways of thinking and behaving. Sometimes these changes create a kind of *peer shock* for the inexperienced teenager. Peer shock is the exposure to people, situations, and ideas—often so foreign to the teenager that they require that teen to make substantial psychological, social, and emotional adjustments. Peer shock can produce an unexpected level of stress. This is normal, and should temper out as the adjustment process progresses.

In some ways, moving from childhood into teenhood is similar to moving to a new city or learning a new language. In many instances, the requirements of the new friendship can impose parallel demands. These and other changes in the lives of teenagers also produce peer shock.

Early childhood "friends" often define their friendship status by proximity and timing. Children tend to seek playmates who live nearby and are available for playtime when they want to play. Teenagers, on the other hand, tend to select their friends based on interests, common beliefs, shared experiences, proximity, and more. When children socialize, they focus on a common activity. When teenagers get together, their relationships are more complex and are centered around mutual trust, loyalty, and commitment.

> "I'm the kind of friend who always listens. People always tell me their troubles, their confidences. I don't have a big mouth. I'll do any favor and not expect anything in return." *(Mayte, 19, Urban)*

> ". . . when homeboys are down with you no matter what, and they never put you down in front of other people." *(Timmy, 17, Urban)*

> "I am a constant friend. I don't radically change my personality or actions on them. I am a loyal friend. I am there until the end, no matter what my friends and I go through. I am a fun friend. I like to be silly and lighthearted." *(Mallie, 18, Urban)*

> "Friendship is a bond between people that allows them to trust, share, and love . . . no matter what happens." *(Sarah, 16, Sub-urban)*

Peer friendships can benefit from peer shock when it encourages or inspires teenagers to develop stronger personal identities and a knowledge of who they are and who they are becoming.

Give and Take

During an extended friendship, each friend will learn to respect the other for many reasons—familiar history, common ideas, shared beliefs. However, if one teen dominates as the giver in the friendship, with the other teen as a constant taker, the relationship will probably self-destruct. Balance and freshness need to prevail in healthy friendships.

> "Everyone wants friends or 'buddies,' but eventually you realize it's more important to have one true friend to help you in times of need. . . . A person you can 'be there for' too." *(Sarah, 18, Rural)*

"Friendship involves the trust, protection, and complete honesty that one or more people give to you and that you give back to them." *(Natasha, 16, Suburban)*

"Friendship has taken on a more emotional aspect. There's less emphasis placed on 'hanging out,' doing things together, and sharing stories. Now there's more emphasis on helping one another through emotionally trying situations." *(Karim, 17, Urban)*

"Friendship used to mean having someone to play with on the playground, but now it means having someone to depend on and someone who depends on you." *(LiAn, 16, Urban)*

EXPANDING FROM ONE FRIEND . . . TO THE GROUP

Each friendship has its own quality, its own distinctiveness. Some friendships are private, one-to-one. They sustain themselves because the two people involved have a special connection that others—outsiders—cannot penetrate.

Other friendships occur in a broader sense and exist only when the people are involved and active in a larger circle of friends. These friendships exist within a complex network, or networks, of friendships. As teenagers constantly redefine who they are, they also experience a transition that affects the way in which they select their friends. These expanded identities help teenagers explore new frontiers of friendship—the Group. I have defined a *group* as three or more individuals who are assembled together and/or have a unifying relationship.

In their teen years, most youths experience a special need for membership in groups. So how do teens and groups connect? How does the selection process begin? How do groups seek out new members? When, why, and how do kids join their groups?

Getting Involved

In most groups, people who get involved often do so because the group is already formed, and it makes itself available to others who are interested in joining. There is no formal "invitation" to belong, no pressure.

Taken to the next level, some groups are more assertive in expanding their membership. Existing members actively seek out potential members and encourage them to join. For example, high school service clubs might have "rush" parties, where they entertain and promote themselves and their club to potential members. Upon joining, these members might be welcomed at an initiation dinner or event.

At the other extreme, gangs sometimes travel to other cities to "recruit" their members. This does not mean that they move their recruits to their own cities; merely, these recruiters help enlist new members. Recruits are often preadolescents, young people with high susceptibility to joining. This susceptibility can occur for many reasons. For example, some children have already been excluded by traditional groups and positive associations. This can occur when they behave in ways adults, including teachers, do not approve, and these adults "label" them as troublemakers. Sometimes youths are excluded because their peers do not understand them, do not want to understand them, or do not give them a chance to be different from the group.

In addition to exclusion, some young people face the harshness of not yet being included. Youths who move often with their families face the challenges of readjustment, including friendship development, that many other young people do not understand. Youths who regularly have to start over in new places can face the struggle of trying to be accepted in friendship circles and activities of those who have lived there longer and already have a shared personal history with their friends. These examples of exclusion and inclusion can result in youths' believing they have limited choices. This can produce in them a vulnerability to be recruited by gangs, which are quite sophisticated in preying on such personal needs.

However, it is important to recognize that many other young people join youth gangs by choice. They are not prompted by exclusion, lack of inclusion, economic hardships, or absence of family. These young people join gangs because they choose to do so.

Once accepted in the youth gang, rather than being the participants in an official and legal event, these members are exposed to violence by being "jumped in"—beaten up by several gang members or forced to commit a crime. This "rite of passage" helps define the nature of the group and its activities.

Friendship Rights

Before taking on a group identity—before being recruited into group membership—teenagers should consider how a particular group will work and answer several personal needs. Teenagers have a right to seek a group that will:

- Have people they can trust and want to call their friends. Teens should ask: Will this group help me meet people I want to know and spend time with?

- Provide opportunities. Teens should ask: Will I be able to share my interests while learning new and useful things when I belong to this group?

- Give them lasting reasons for staying in the group. Teens should ask: Will I grow and become a better person because of my ongoing membership in this group?

- Equip them with the tools to deal with different situations and people in various environments. Teens should ask: Will I learn how to interact effectively with other group members, even when we do not always agree?

- Balance the needs of the individual with the needs of the group. Teens should ask: Will the group move forward with its own purpose and still respect my personal needs for growth and individuality?

- Inspire them to make contributions. Teens should ask: Will my being a member of this group empower me to make a difference in this group and elsewhere?

Of course, new friends and group membership do not require drastic moves into new environments. Sometimes, change involves the mere exchange of one friend for another, or the evolutionary step from a single friend into a group. With group membership comes the expansion of the friendship circle and the safety of numbers. Whatever the chosen route, this movement helps define a process of self-discovery for teenagers. Through this process, adolescents can present themselves as they are becoming, not as they have been.

THE SEARCH FOR PEER APPROVAL

One of the greatest pursuits for teenagers is that of *peer approval*. Teen agendas focus on the drive to be accepted, and to look appropriate to people they want to impress—their peers.

As teenagers separate from their parents, they hungrily search for friends—groups—who welcome them and offer a ready support system. To teenagers this often represents their first independent experience with the outside world, so success at this level can be extremely important.

Peer Pressure

Peer pressure means being influenced, convinced, or talked into doing or not doing something by friends. The matter of "pressure" implies, at least in some instances, that the teenagers are being forced in a way that goes against their true feelings or values. Groups often pressure their members to conform to the group's ideas and desires. This sometimes might diverge from the individual teenager's ideas or wishes. Often this pressure occurs with risk-taking behaviors like smoking, drinking, taking drugs, and engaging in sexual relations. Thirty-five percent of the youths surveyed for this book indicated that "peer approval" was a primary need they had when selecting a group. Yet only eleven percent considered "peer pressure" a reason for associating with their current group of friends.

Parents often worry about their children's choice of friends. They concern themselves with the "bad" influences that will prevail in their teens' lives. They fret that their children will make the wrong friends and do the wrong things. These and similar concerns often prompt battles between parents and teens and can create unnecessary ill feelings. Ironically, when teenagers select their own friends, they learn how to deal with all kinds of people and diverse relationships. Thirty-one percent of surveyed youths belong to a particular group because they consider it "the best group for my needs." Complementing this sentiment, more than half of the youths join a particular group because they "feel comfortable with the other group members."

> "My mother wants me to pick new friends all the time. This is not because she doesn't like the ones I have, but because she wants me to have a selection or variety. She has never forced me to be a friend to any particular person or join any particular group." *(Mary, 16, Suburban)*

> "My parents tend to evaluate my friends. However, when I evaluate theirs, they are offended. They want my friends to be honorable." *(Michael, 16, Urban)*

> "They don't influence whom I pick as friends, and they don't tell me how my friends should act. If they did, I would have a serious talk with them." *(Natalie, 17, Urban)*

"My parents don't want my friends to be gang members. They want them to be good friends who don't get in trouble." *(Jessie, 14, Inner City)*

"My mom really doesn't tell me what she wants my friends to be like, just as long as they don't get me in any more trouble than usual." *(Christine, 16, Suburban)*

Dealing with Negative Peer Pressure

To deal with negative peer pressure, teenagers need to recognize their own self-worth. By accepting their experiences and relationships for what they are and how they can contribute to personal development, teenagers can turn this knowledge into learning experiences. These lessons can help teenagers empower themselves to avoid negative peer pressure and to excel in personal development.

Another way of dealing with negative peer pressure encourages teenagers to think ahead. They should ask themselves:

- What might happen if I give in by doing or not doing something that the group is pressing me about?
- What might happen if I do not succumb to peer pressure?
- How will I feel about myself afterward?
- What can I expect from other people if I do or do not give in to peer pressure?
- Could I get into trouble if I do what the group is pressuring me to do or not to do?
- Am I willing to "pay the price" for listening to and acting the way the group wants me to act?

Certainly adolescent growth requires a healthy involvement with people who can offer other members of the group diversity of thought, attitude, experience, and action. Membership cloning has the potential to stunt individual development. Teens need to weigh the opinions, ideas, and actions of their group.

THE MERGING PROCESS

When teenagers move into the group-friendship stage of their lives, they often move into a process of *merging* with their friends. In some ways, they become interchangeable with each other. They see themselves in each other and cling to these mirrored images of themselves. This reflection provides a source of security.

Personal Safety Zones Offer Protection

A primary reason for teen membership in groups centers around *safety*. Teenagers seek the comfort of others and the protection they offer. The teen years provide enough turbulence—friends help friends survive.

In this search, teenagers look for personal *safety zones*. A safety zone can be any place or activity—mental or physical—that gives teenagers comfort and a sense of security. This can be a basketball court, a room, a favorite hangout, as well as studying a favorite subject, attending an aerobics class, or talking on the telephone with a friend.

Groups often provide teenagers with the insulation of a safety zone. The support of friends, and the comfort they provide, reassures teenagers that they are welcome and have people—the group—to take them in and shelter them from the outside. Thirty-eight percent of youths surveyed joined their groups for "refuge."

Groups have the ability to substitute a new source of security for that safety the teenager enjoyed—or should have enjoyed—at home. The members of the group provide nurturing and support to help fill the void its teenage members might experience while testing their personal safety zones. During this pursuit for new experiences, adolescents learn about their own potential, and they learn to define what is important to them. Also, with the assistance and often the encouragement of the group, they learn which risks are worthwhile in their efforts to excel.

Teenagers can also recognize through this experience when they are involved with the wrong group. This often occurs when they find themselves wanting to "get away" from the group—when they would rather be almost anywhere else, doing anything else, rather than spending time with these people.

For teenagers to grow they need to challenge their safety zones, otherwise their safety zones will actually shrink and disappear. To ensure that the safety zone survives, teenagers need to overcome their fears of the unknown and the undone. Of course, this requires venturing beyond what is comfortable to experience new and different things—those things teenagers might otherwise be afraid to do, or might think they are unable to accomplish.

Clothing, Symbols, and Music

Teenage groups adopt certain distinctive symbols to describe who they are and why they are different from others. One way to accomplish this identity is through clothing. Teenagers today are more vocal than ever about what they will and will not wear. While one group might wear the " '70s retro look," another group might wear baggy jeans and oversized T-shirts. Still another group might identify itself from outsiders through jewelry, such as pins, necklaces, earrings, and bracelets, or with accessories like belts, hats, and sunglasses. Even haircuts and gestures distinguish groups. On a more permanent level, some groups denote their membership with "body art" that can involve tattooing, piercing, and even branding.

> "These 'signs' are important so you know just by looking at someone what they are into." *(Chris, 17, Urban)*

> "We know our homeboys because of our blue rags, hair nets, and the way we wear our pants." *(Jeremy, 17, Inner City)*

> "In 4-H we wear green ties, white shirts, and dark or black jeans. It shows people that we are with the 4-H, and gives them good impressions." *(Cara, 15, Rural)*

Language

Language serves as another identifying factor in and for the group. As children move into adolescence, their language will take on a new life—that of their peers, their group. In fact, language can take on its own degree of "secrecy" as teens learn to create an exclusivity with their intragroup communications.

> "It's important that we speak our own language to each other and share our common goals and cultures." *(Africa, 19, Inner City)*

> "I tend to adapt, yet I never dishonor my code of conduct. Every group has slang and, in order to be part of a group, you must adapt." *(Michael, 16, Urban)*

Some teens want to avoid isolating themselves in such overt ways:

> "If I took on the ideas, slang, and attitudes of a group, then I'd lose my own sense of who I am." *(Chris, 17, Urban)*

> "Keeping your own identity is a big thing. Having someone else's is stupid." *(Stephanie, 14, Urban)*

> "I will take on a group's ideas and attitudes if they are similar to mine, but I will not take on the ideas and attitudes if they change what I really feel." *(LiAn, 16, Urban)*

Shared Interests and Activities

When teenagers look for friendships, they often search for common interests first. For the shared interest to provide staying power for group members, however, their commitment to that interest or activity must be genuine. Faking an interest in something, just for the sake of being a member of that group, will not withstand time and the other demands a group can impose on its members.

Some teenagers do not have the option to join clubs or other organized activities. These teenagers go to work instead, holding part-time jobs during high school. This employment often preempts traditional group involvement for them. Many working teenagers, however, take advantage of the workplace to build lasting friendships. With their co-workers they might share after-work activities, recreational interests, or career goals. Working teenagers have their own ways to build lasting friendships, many of which will grow with them into adulthood. Seventy-five percent of the youths surveyed for this book indicated "shared activities, time, and place" as primary reasons for forming their friendship groups.

Time Together

Teenagers who enjoy their group membership want to spend time together. In the early stages, belonging to a group requires special nurturing. One of the best ways to accomplish this involves sharing time with each other.

Shared time reinforces closeness and support—two of the driving forces for joining a group in the first place. Sharing time also means that friends make themselves available for one other. They "are there" for each other when the need arises. I often call these friends my "2:00 A.M. friends." These are the people I can call, and who can call me, at 2:00 A.M., and they know that we will be available to each other for any reason or purpose.

Some adolescents, however, need more "alone" time than others. They prefer to avoid the "crowding" that contact with others might impose. This does not mean that they do not enjoy their friendships, but that they prefer less group time.

> "I used to want people to hang out with, something to do, something to occupy time. Now I like to be alone, or at home. My friends are those with whom I enjoy the time we spend together. A close friend is someone who knows my heart, my feelings, and my personality . . . always." *(Mallie, 18, Urban)*

Place and Space

Teenagers who want to get the most from their groups also need places to share time with them. This sharing of time, place, and activities gives teenagers better opportunities to enhance their emotional connections.

> "Sharing interests with my friends is important. If we have nothing in common, then why spend time with them?" *(LiAn, 16, Urban)*

> "My friends and I have what we call 'bum time' together, when we just hang around someone's house and talk. We share secrets, braid hair, and take time out from our busy lives for each other." *(Kristy, 17, Suburban)*

> "When I am by myself I don't feel as confident about myself as I do when I'm with my friends. My friends cheer me up and make me feel good about myself, and this helps us get along better with everyone." *(Kassi, 14, Rural)*

Of course, doing things together can serve a purpose. But it is also important for teenagers to budget time that does nothing more than provide fun. Teenagers need play time, in the same way their parents find recreation critical to their own search for balanced lives.

Multigroup Membership

Some teenagers prefer not to belong to just one group, because this limits their choices. Multigroup membership also prevents teenagers from getting too narrowly focused on their interests and their selection of friends.

> "I spend a lot of time in many different groups. I usually hang around with well put-together, intelligent, popular people." *(Joshua, 17, Urban)*

> "I have many friends who like me. I hang around with many people. I like to get involved with whatever or whomever I can." *(Charla, 15, Suburban)*

> "I 'belong' to several groups. I spend the most time with the group that I have known for a long period of time, because we know how each of us feels about important things." *(Kassi, 14, Rural)*

No Groups

Of course, some teens do *not belong* to a group at all. Maybe they decide not to participate in groups because they prefer their solitude, or they cannot find a group that satisfies their needs. Sometimes they avoid joining groups because they are rebelling, and this helps them deny what others expect of them.

> "I find it hard to stick with a certain type of people. I love to mingle and meet a lot of different people." *(Moria, 16, Urban)*

> "I don't like anyone telling me where or where not to go. I like to be free and have all kinds of friends and not just one particular set of people." *(Nereyda, 17, Urban)*

Other teens are *non*-members of groups, because no particular group accepts them. This can create painful feelings in teenagers who are treated as outsiders. Some teenagers respond to this situation by creating new avenues for associations with others. They also might look to diversity, rather than similarity, as a criterion for friendship selection. This encourages opportunities for inclusion, rather than exclusion.

Whatever the scenario, it is critical for all children to realize that they have choices about whom they select as friends. Acting on this awareness—and the empowerment it ensures—will significantly and positively impact their lives. When they accept that they have the right to choose their own friends, young people exercise personal power, confidence in themselves. They are "in control" of their lives, not "being controlled" by others who do not have the same appreciation of friendship. One simple point they should remember in creating their own healthy friendship: Friends help each other be the best they can be!

> "In my neighborhood I just have to stick to my own. My group helps me go beyond this . . . to meet other people from all races and cultures, and to make friends with people unlike me." *(Mayte, 19, Urban)*

> "People who are not members of my group are carefully examined and tested before they are accepted. This type of treatment bugs me, and I try to be more open." *(Jonathan, 17, Suburban)*

Chapter Highlights

- In their early searches for independence from their parents, teenagers experience a degree of uncertainty and fear.
- Friendship, which always fluctuates, offers teenagers exposure to new ways of thinking and acting.
- Requirements imposed by new friendships create stress for teenagers. This can result in *peer shock*.
- As teenagers constantly redefine their identities, they also move into new ways to select their friends. They explore new frontiers of friendship—the Group.
- A *group* is defined as three or more individuals who are assembled together and/or have a unifying relationship.
- Recruitment of teenagers for membership in a group will vary from group to group.
- Teenagers have a right to seek a group based on several criteria. The teen should ask:

    —Does the group have people I can trust and will want to call my friends?

    —Will group membership provide me with opportunities?

—Will the group give me lasting reasons for staying in the group?

—Will the group help me deal with different situations and people in various environments?

—Will the group balance my needs with the needs of the group?

—Will the group inspire me to make contributions?

- One of a teenager's greatest searches is for *peer approval*.

- As teenagers separate from their parents, they turn to their friends—groups—for their support system.

- *Peer pressure* means being influenced, convinced, or talked into doing or not doing something by friends.

- When teenagers move into the group-friendship stage of their lives, they often move into a process of *merging* with their friends.

- A primary reason for group membership centers around *safety*. Teenagers seek the comfort of others—outside of the home—and the protection they provide.

- As teenagers expand the dimensions of their personal *safety zones*, they develop more power and control over their lives.

- Teenage groups adopt distinctive symbols to describe who they are and why they are different from others. Obvious demonstrations of membership can include clothing, symbols, and taste in music.

- Language also helps identify group membership, especially in gangs.

- When teenagers share the same interests and like the same things, they take a giant step toward building friendship in their group.

- Some teenagers—often those who work part time—do not have the option to join clubs or organized activities, but experience benefits from the employment experience.

- Group membership also involves sharing time and space. Some members, however, prefer more "alone" time and space than others.

- Some teens prefer to belong to more than one circle of friends. Others avoid group membership because they prefer solitude, cannot find the right group, or are not accepted by a particular group.

- Children of all ages must realize that they have choices about who they select as friends. Acting on this awareness will significantly impact their lives.

Chapter 3

Power in a Youth's Life

Individually relying on oneself
To concentrate on action,
A person with responsibility
Fulfills the obligation.

Realizing only one's character
Can develop the dedication,
A person with responsibility
Promotes cooperation.

Taking the opportunity for growth
And providing compassion,
A person with responsibility
Gains inner satisfaction.

Distinguishing right from wrong
To create a decision,
A person with responsibility
Leads with no hesitation.

Neil, 17, Inner City

POWER AND AUTHORITY

The push and pull of the adolescent years often peaks with a *struggle for power*, a time when teenagers presume that they have no dominion over their own lives. They believe that all decisions, important or not, come from a "higher power"—parents, teachers, even peers. Sometimes this is true. But often it results from forfeiture, the giving up of responsible decision making.

As teenagers progress through their adolescence, one of the major adjustments they experience revolves around *authority*. Their need to understand the impact of authority involves the role that parents and other adults play in their lives. Equally important for teens is their peer group—and, eventually, themselves.

Control: From the Parents' Perspective

Though most teenagers demonstrate responsibility in making decisions for themselves, they sometimes lack the consistent ability to make long-term decisions. They ponder the choices, and they know that they can turn to their parents or their friends. The group provides a sanctuary, where teens can soften the impact of parental wrath and authoritarianism.

The vast majority of teens still need to go home at some point and respond to their parents or caregivers. Sometimes it takes a while, but teens generally recognize that their parents have something of value to say. They also accept, at least momentarily, their parents' assertion of authority. Knowing this, parents should respect their teenagers' abilities to understand the parameters of parental authority.

Parents also should help their teens learn how to adapt their own thinking and values to daily living. This will help teenagers learn how to mature into adult decision makers, with the ability to live by their own decisions.

As teenagers get older, they tend to have a better understanding of what parents and other people of authority expect of them. They learn how to adapt their own behavior with what is "socially and legally acceptable." Yet they also learn how to carve out their own identities and independence. This comprises an important aspect of their own personal evolution.

Parenting Styles Influence Teenagers

The style of parenting determines the kind of relationship parents will have with their children, especially when it comes to defining and delineating authority. Teenagers, in turn, learn these styles and apply them to their own behavior within their groups. After all, most of what they initially learn is learned at home.

According to Don Fleming, author of *How to Stop the Battle with Your*

Teenager (1989), *overcritical* parents believe that they can teach their teenagers about life by telling them everything they are doing wrong. Unfortunately, this usually results in the teenager's hatred of the parent's voice and opinions. Also, parents who constantly tell their teenagers how incompetent they are impose feelings of helplessness and inability on their teens. What impact does this have on teens and their friends? Overcritical offspring sometimes become overcritical friends. They might tend to look for what is wrong with their friends, not what is right.

Other parenting styles can wreak comparable havoc in teenagers' lives. *Combative* parents lose both verbal control and authority. Frequently, these parents do not know their teenagers. Yet they think they are teaching their teenagers about life and values. Of course, combative parents also believe that their teenagers should accept these opinions without question or argument. But arguments inevitably ensue. How do teens translate their parents' behavior into their relationships with their group? They often create and perpetuate arguments within their groups, which puts additional and unnecessary stress into the mix.

Some want to be *friendly* parents. These parents tend to be overly tolerant, demonstrating little or no authority. They accept most of their teenagers' behavior and want to add a "pal" element to the fun times and conversations. Unfortunately, by relinquishing their authority, these parents also avoid setting necessary limits and boundaries. Their teenagers discover these restrictions for themselves. Teenagers still need adults in their lives, which might prompt them to look outside the home for adult guidance. For example, they might lean exclusively on their group to help them make important decisions.

Parents who assert *too* much control—*authoritarian* parents—send a clear message to their teenagers: "I'm the boss, so what I say goes." Many parents rely on this style because they have had problems with their teenagers, and they feel that this is their only parenting choice. However, overcontrolling parents tend to overlook their teenager's struggle for independence and opportunities to express other feelings. This form of parenting can damage the teenager and the relationship between parent and child. Again, the group might fill the void as a "family that cares" for the teen and, in return, as a teen who cares for the "family."

Some parents assert their authority over their teenagers by becoming *outrageous*. They respond to behavior that they do not like by throwing temper tantrums or blowing their cool. Their teenagers take the brunt of these reactions. By overreacting, outrageous parents lose contact with their teenagers. Teens learn to ignore or tune out their parents' words and behavior, as evidenced by some of the antisocial behavior in this country. Teenagers often mimic their parents' hostile behaviors, especially when they see so much of it at home. In anger and frustration, these teenagers often turn to groups that demonstrate similar behaviors and forms of control over others.

Absent parents reflect the times. They do not share a lot of time or activity with their teenagers. By circumstance or by choice, these parents commit little time to parenting, yet hope that their teenagers will be mature enough to "figure it out for themselves." What results? Teenagers who tend to resent rules, reject structure, and have difficulty with the growing-up process. More and more teens live in homes where parents appear—and disappear—with regularity. So what part does the group play? These teens often reach out to their groups to fill the parental void. They know that they can seek out their friends to fill the lost time, the lost activity, the lost input.

There also are parents who recognize and appreciate the value of *responsible* parenting. They want to assert themselves as the adults, the parents, in their families. They set proper limits and monitor their teenagers. As their teenagers mature, these parents respect their children's evolution and ability to make decisions for themselves. They trust their children to the degree that their teenagers demonstrate respect and responsibility. They know when to talk, and when to listen. Responsible parents communicate openly with their children and invite their teenagers to be assertive and responsible. *Consistency* serves as a watchword for these parents. Teens from these families have the opportunity to develop healthy friendships and to enhance their groups.

Whatever parenting style adults adopt will directly impact the teenager. It will also affect the teenager's group—the friends who not only offer support through the growing-up years, but who also experience parenting styles in their own homes. These parenting choices will influence teenagers in the ways in which they react to conflict, praise, punishment, reward, goal setting, and more, and to the other people in their lives, particularly their friends.

INDEPENDENCE, AUTONOMY, AND ALL THAT STUFF

During adolescence, teenagers experience mixed feelings about their independence. Sometimes they want their parents, teachers, and other adults in their lives to make decisions and be responsible for them. At other times, teens resent their own dependency on their parents. This occurs especially when parents encourage their children's dependence on them—including everything from giving their teens rides to school to granting them permission to go to parties.

It is normal for adolescents to crave independence. It is normal for them to want enough space to make their own decisions. It is normal for them to want choices in matters that affect their lives. It is normal for them to want to use sources outside the home. It is normal for them to resent being bombarded with too many questions. And it is normal for them to be confused about, and struggle with, the role of their parents—the primary authorities in their lives.

All of this is normal, especially when it comes to the selection of friends. Forty-five percent of surveyed youths said their parents have "very little" or "no" influence over their own choice of friends. Of course, in comparison, fifty-five percent said their parents have "some" or "very much" influence on those they choose as friends!

No one would question the reality that teenagers are positioned in the middle of a revolution—their own miniwar. They are struggling with who they were as children, who others expect them to be as teenagers, and who they want to become as adults. Teenagers are immersed in a push and pull—a tug-of-war—that can leave them feeling frustrated and angry. Fortunately, they are not alone. Their friends are also experiencing this personal earthquake.

Most adolescents will spend their teen years searching for their most prized possession: their personal identities. During these years, most parents make a great effort to prepare their adolescents for the future. However, simultaneously, teenagers will do everything they can to do things their own way, again the demands of a dual identity. Often, many of the steps teens take will be in a particular direction for the first time.

THE CHALLENGES OF MISBEHAVIOR

While traveling on new paths, adolescents will make a lot of mistakes and discover many new ways to improve their self-esteem when it is challenged. Along the way, however, some of their choices will produce negative returns such as misbehavior—and sometimes even delinquency.

According to Bob Myers in his book *Parenting Teenagers in the 1990s* (1992), it is important to understand behavior in terms of reasons, causes, and purposes. Myers asserts that a *reason* can be thought of as the "why"—whatever it is that motivates the behavior. The reason stems either from a *cause*—something in the past which led to the behavior—or for a *purpose*—

something that is to be gained from, or avoided by, the behavior in the future.

Children, from their earliest stages of development, act to satisfy some need or want. They use whatever methods that have worked in the past to gain that satisfaction.

Reasons for Misbehavior

Misbehavior derives from four primary sources: attention, revenge, inadequacy, and power. For parents and other adults to resolve the child's misbehavior, they need to understand why the child is acting out in a negative way. They can do this by taking note of what feelings have been stirred up, and by being aware of the child's continued attempts to stir up those feelings again.

Attention. If the feeling that the teen prompts in the parents is annoyance, and the parental response incites additional annoying behavior, the child is probably trying to get attention. The best thing to do is ignore the behavior, because reinforcing "attention on demand" can produce unwanted results, and quite often.

Revenge. The purpose of the teen's behavior is probably revenge if his or her actions make the parent want to strike back or get even. The parent's response to reciprocate will usually prompt further misbehavior. One reason for revenge is the child's frustration or feeling of resentment about the unevenness of power in the relationship. Giving children, especially teenagers, more say in making decisions about things that affect them might help even up the problem.

Inadequacy. When the parent feels inadequate, helpless, or powerless in response to the child's behavior—and this prompts more misbehavior of the same kind—the chances are the teen also feels inadequate and helpless. Ironically, teens with these feelings will often pass off the responsibility for this misbehavior to anyone or anything else. To resolve this, the youth must assume responsibility for his or her personal actions by accepting the consequences of them.

Power Struggles

Actions. Reactions. It is as simple, or as difficult, as that. The one behavior that parents, adults, and teens can control is their own response to what others do. This is real power.

Unfortunately, when issues between parents and their teens escalate, often it seems that one wins and the other one loses. Realistically, though, both lose, because anything of that intensity will damage the relationship. The only way to successfully handle a power struggle is to take charge of the situation by backing off. For parents, this means taking control by removing themselves from the conflict and from the status as their child's competitor.

The same applies to teens with their peers. No relationship survives angry competition. Three options that can help adults and teens—and teens and teens—resolve their power struggles are:

1. State their own opinions and state what they intend to do about the situation. They must refuse to argue about it.
2. State their opinion and explain that they are willing to talk about it when the other person is willing to listen. Then they should withdraw until that time.
3. State that they are willing to agree to disagree. This takes practice and stamina.

RESOLVING PEER CONFLICT

Often the struggle for personal power results in conflict. When conflict, however complex, arises in friendship, both friends need to seek resolution as soon as possible. By letting tempers simmer, or misunderstandings brew, friends test their friendship in unhealthy, preventable ways.

Teenagers also need to realize that they have the right not to agree with their friends. A crucial part of friendship involves recognizing the differences, as well as the similarities, that drew them together in the first place, especially when they are handling conflict. By resolving conflict, friends do not need to determine a right and wrong person or point of view. Such resolution requires each friend to share information honestly with the other. It also compels each friend to resolve the problem. Solid friendships reinforce these opportunities and the growth of the friendship that results.

> ". . . from sharing toys to counseling crises. As a teenager, most of my friendships are now formed with the purpose of consulting in a crisis situation." *(Michael, 16, Urban)*

> "I hang out with them a lot more, and I think it's harder to keep friends than when you were a little kid. Tough times require tough actions." *(Jason, 17, Inner City)*

"Friends used to be people to play with. Now they're people who grow up with you and accept you, even if you have hang-ups between you." *(Chris, 17, Urban)*

A powerful way to resolve conflicts, misunderstandings, and tensions incorporates a four-part communication formula. The "When you–I feel–because–I prefer" approach to conflict resolution helps teens during tough times.

- *"When you* . . ." The teen states a particular disturbing behavior. For example, "When you decide what we're going to do on a Friday night without asking me . . ."
- *"I feel* . . ." The teen specifies an emotional response. "I feel disappointed and cheated."
- *"Because* . . ." The teen describes in enough detail why this action arouses these particular feelings. "Because you choose activities that I often do not enjoy."
- *"I prefer* . . ." The teen explains a preferred replacement behavior that the friend should adopt. "I prefer that you include me in the planning so that I know my ideas and interests are important to you."

Accountability

The bonds of friendship thrive on a sense of generosity and mutuality. Friends are givers, listeners, and respecters. Friendship does not survive when it is formed around wins and losses. It does, however, require *accountability.* When teenagers realize that they must think and act accountably, they recognize that they are involved in an active process. They know that they have options, as well as the ability, to act on their choices for action.

Therefore, teenagers who practice friendship honestly do not blame others for what happens to them. They do not get angry at their parents for not doing for them what they can do for themselves. They do not expect things to "just happen." Yes, even in the best of times, teenagers—like adults— "slip" and blame others, just to relieve themselves from the pressure that making mistakes imposes. However, this finger-pointing does not work.

Friendship practitioners know that they have the ability to make things happen. Responsible adolescents realize that when they act and react accountably, someone—even if it is only themselves—has placed enough trust in them to see it through. By being honest with themselves first, adolescents learn to count on themselves first. This reduces the pressure of counting on their friends to solve their problems, which is often an impossible task anyway.

Forgiving Friends

When teen friends disappoint each other, bruised emotions often result. When friends store mental junk about each other, it can place stumbling blocks in the way of the friendship. To resolve and recover, friends need to learn the art and skill of *forgiveness*.

Deciding to forgive a friend is a choice. Other choices include anger and disappointment. When teenagers select negative options, the friendship can suffer. By choosing to forgive, friends replace the desire to hold on to anger with the greater desire to maintain an important relationship. By preferring to forgive, teens put aside pride, admit that they have done something—however slight—that is wrong or improper, and become willing to move forward with the friendship.

Another antagonist that can stand in the way of forgiveness is *guilt*. Real guilt—for real errors—has the power, though, to provide positive results. It can challenge teenagers to *seek* forgiveness. Unfortunately, guilt most often prompts teenagers to stand in their own way. It creates a reluctance within teens to forgive themselves. Therefore, in dealing with forgiveness, teenagers should:

- Forgive friends and learn to forgive themselves first.
- Carefully evaluate lofty expectations and standards and consider whether they are expecting too much of themselves and others.
- Shed the form of guilt that serves as a patterned response to life itself.
- Forgive themselves and believe in themselves without the entanglement of unnecessary guilt.
- Set aside ill feelings about themselves and others and be willing to act in spite of those potentially debilitating feelings.
- Act now, rather than wait for the right opportunity to offer forgiveness to themselves and others.

The search for power, which starts from within each teenager as an exploration for independence, can be a long, difficult struggle, or it can be a personal enhancement. The choices for managing this necessary challenge are as many and as individual as the teenager who takes advantage of them.

Chapter Highlights

- The push and pull of the adolescent years often peaks with a *struggle for power*.

- As teenagers progress through adolescence, one of their major adjustments revolves around *authority*.

- Teenagers generally make appropriate decisions for themselves, but they sometimes lack the consistent ability to make long-term decisions.

- The *parenting style* helps determine the kind of relationship that parents have with their children, especially when it comes to defining and delineating authority.

- Parenting styles include, but are not limited to: *overcritical, combative, friendly, authoritarian, outrageous, absent,* and *responsible*.

- During adolescence, teenagers experience mixed feelings about their independence.

- Most teenagers will spend their teen years searching for their most prized possession: their personal identities.

- It is important to understand behavior in terms of *reasons, causes,* and *purposes*.

- Misbehavior derives from four primary sources: *attention, revenge, inadequacy,* and *power*.

- Often the struggle for personal power results in conflict—even with peers.

- Teenagers need to realize that they have the right not to agree with their friends.

- Bonds of friendship thrive on a sense of generosity and mutuality. Friendship does not survive when based on wins and losses.

- By forgiving friends, teens choose not to hold on to anger; instead, they prefer to maintain an important relationship.

- Guilt, though often an antagonistic response, can challenge teenagers to seek forgiveness.

Part II

The Gang Life

Chapter 4

From the Beginning

Something you have or you don't.
When it comes time, you will or you won't.
You have to check deep inside
When there's a brawl, will you run or hide?

Do you have the guts to be a man?
When it is all over, say, "I could have, but I ran."
If no one is there and your back is against the wall,
Will you shrink like a midget or be like a giant and stand big
    and tall?

In the heat of a battle, and a friend is hit,
Do you leave him there for the enemy and try to forget?
No, you go back and get him, no matter what it takes.
The consequences are irrelevant, even though it might be a
    mistake.

If a family member is drowning, and you have to go deep,
Your courageous effort, and the fact you tried, is what you can
    keep.
To me, these are characteristics a man must possess.
So when it is all over, he will have something called courage
    . . . no more, no less.

Will, 17, Inner City

THE HISTORY OF AMERICAN GANGS

Ganglike activity is not new to this country, nor is its impact. The first known organized gang was formed in the back of a small grocery store in New York City in 1826. Even then, gangs had distinctive clothing, language, and identity.

Early American gangs divided themselves primarily along ethnic, racial, and cultural lines. Two other important considerations in the historic development of gangs were urbanization and poverty.

Some of the earliest gangs began as *friendship groups*. Members were committed to protecting themselves and their neighborhood. Then, as now, gangs served as social connectors when other institutions failed. Many of these gangs evolved to form major crime syndicates during and after Prohibition in the 1920s. Gang wars often erupted as each gang asserted itself to control specific territories and illegal activities, especially the production and sale of illegal alcohol, bookmaking, extortion, and gunrunning.

During the Depression and World War II, gangs declined and few people paid attention to them. In the 1930s and 1940s, European-derived gangs still had a strong presence in this country. By the end of World War II, America had experienced rapid social change—and a surge in modern gang activity—as the U.S. economy struggled to adapt to peacetime. At this time, African-American—especially those moving from the south to the north for jobs and opportunities—Puerto Rican, and Mexican-American gangs gained power, especially in the northern cities.

In the 1950s, gang warfare between African-American and Hispanic gangs peaked in cities such as Chicago, New York, Detroit, Boston, Philadelphia, and Los Angeles. These "battles" erupted because of racial differences, turf disputes, and illegal activities. Often such battles manifested their frustrations from *status goals*: wanting the "American Dream" and not being able to attain it—legally.

During the 1960s, national attention was focused on the Vietnam War, civil rights, and urban riots. As people were concerned about the nation's political agenda, gang membership dipped. In the 1970s, political unrest prompted the immigration of more than one million Asian refugees to the United States. Both language and socioeconomic barriers inspired them to form Southeast Asian gangs. As the Vietnam War began to unwind, gangs—African-American, Caucasian, and Hispanic—began to reemerge.

At the same time, the media began a trend toward more overt violence, and newer gangs mirrored this change. With this new self-image and access to more sophisticated, deadly weaponry, gang conflicts became more violent. The Crips and the Bloods—the nation's largest gangs—took form, and several of these gangs started their movement toward a national status.

THE BIG CHALLENGE: DEFINING GANGS

The diversity of groups that the term *gang* has been used to define demonstrates how difficult it is to address the gang problem. Certainly, because adolescents spend so much of their time in groups, it is important to distinguish between legitimate activities and illegal ones.

It is essential at the outset, therefore, to distinguish between gangs and groups. In the first three chapters of this book, I described what most, if not all, youths seek from their groups. The group experience is a familiar and normal phenomenon in an adolescent's life, with a typical emphasis on being together and belonging to something. Fifty-one percent of the youths surveyed for this book indicated that "belonging" is a primary need that they want their group to satisfy for them. Gangs, however, represent an extreme—and often an illegal—manifestation of these peer connections, expectations, and experiences.

Youth Gangs

In an attempt to find a workable definition for this book, we will use the term *youth gang*. By necessity, this means that we will not be addressing the issues of adult drug, prison, street, social, violent, delinquent, motorcycle, and other kinds of *activity-defined gangs*. Although youths may engage in some or many of these activities within a gang, their gangs are not defined by one of these activities.

Youth gangs consist of adolescents and young adults—usually from ages twelve to twenty-five—who share a collective identity. They usually express this identity through a name, language, and symbols unique to their gang. They are generally territorial—they control their *turf*—and often they have been raised in neighborhoods where other members and generations of their families have held gang memberships. They also repeatedly engage in illegal activities. According to nationally recognized gang expert Dr. James C. "Buddy" Howell, youth gangs also have identifiable leadership and continuous association and interaction. In addition, youth gangs want to prove themselves, establish a reputation, and be recognized for their activities, as evidenced by the comments that follow:

> ". . . a group of people who don't feel they belong—or are rejected. They turn to each other and a negative lifestyle for that sense of belonging and to get revenge." *(Lynn, 20, Rural)*

". . . a kick-back group of mischief who are insecure in themselves. They try to fit in and enforce power by violence and make others pay for what someone else did to them." *(Nereyda, 17, Urban)*

". . . a group of teenagers who unite for support but have few, if any, morals and continuously break the law." *(John, 16, Rural)*

". . . not a social club. They are violent and destructive. They try to change people by threatening them, and only learn later that these people retaliate." *(Danna, 17, Urban)*

". . . young people who are very dangerous or violent at times. They harm people even if they don't know them. They have no respect for society or others." *(Kristi, 16, Rural)*

". . . a group of youths who join together to form an almost alternate family, shunning outsiders and sometimes causing problems." *(Sarah, 16, Suburban)*

". . . a group of soldiers who are down for each other." *(Vinnie, 17, Inner City)*

". . . soul searchers who are mentally lost youths, looking for love or belonging from the wrong group. Physically, they are attached to one color of dress, talk slang, wear heavy makeup. In one word . . . raunchy!" *(Serena, 17, Urban)*

". . . a family in the street." *(Brandon, 16, Suburban)*

". . . a group of individuals who are lost and seeking support and a sense of something—anything. A youth gang fits into the community the same way a square peg fits into a round hole." *(Russ, 18, Inner City)*

When asked to describe a "typical" youth gang member, survey participants had different ideas:

"An insecure kid in denial." *(Spencer, 16, Urban)*

". . . destructive, wild, protective, hard-headed, hurt." *(Candice, 17, Inner City)*

". . . someone who looks as if he or she is strong and powerful but is really lost and alone." *(Russ, 18, Inner City)*

". . . selfish, conceited, arrogant, scared, and obsessive." *(Matthew, 17, Urban)*

". . . a person who doesn't feel loved or accepted and turns to the streets." *(Lucas, 15, Rural)*

"There is no 'typical youth gang member.' The media describe them as troublemakers, looking to harm someone. Peers describe them as kids who need to be loved and given a chance." *(Tonya, 17, Rural)*

"There is no such thing as 'typical youth gang members.' There are only stereotypes." *(Mario, 17, Inner City)*

TYPES OF GANGS

Gangs originally formed along ethnic and racial lines. Now, many gangs are ethnically diverse. In fact, today, economic incentives often are the decisive consideration in joining a gang.

Hispanic Gangs

Hispanic gangs first developed in this country in the early 1900s. They formed small, loosely knit neighborhood groups. In the 1930s and 1940s, they organized to protect themselves from outside influences, including criminals and unwelcome government or law enforcement.

These ethnic gangs cling very closely to their Old World culture and heritage. This also underscores their devout loyalty to their neighborhoods or turf.

Hispanic gang members tend to have a single-minded devotion to their gang and its members, the "to die for" kind of loyalty. Unlike most other ethnic gangs, they totally immerse themselves in their gang activities. They commit similar drug-related crimes as black gangs, and they participate in other crimes of violence as well.

Hispanic gangs, which cater to eleven-to-twenty-five-year-olds, primarily include Mexican-American, Puerto Rican, Dominican, and Salvadoran groups. Some of these gangs have more than three or four generations of family involvement, which helps reinforce the sense of continuity of family identity. They are known primarily by their tattoos, hand signs, and graffiti.

Hispanic youths are more likely than most other gangs to be integrated into multiethnic and multiracial gangs, probably because they generally reside in more mixed neighborhoods. It is also important to note that large numbers of first- and second-generation Mexican-American youths find ways to move out of the barrios to become a part of the larger society.

Black Gangs

African-American or *black gangs* began in the 1920s as nonviolent, loose associations. However, through the decades, legitimate opportunities have often been denied to urban African Americans. Because of these ongoing denials, substantial systems of illegitimate opportunity have evolved. Today, most black members, ranging from ages eleven to thirty-five, are affiliated with either the Crips—identified by their color blue—or the rival Bloods—known by their color red—the two most violent and criminally active African-American gangs in the country. They are well known for their drug trafficking.

Two other prominent affiliations—considered *gang nations*—are the Folks and the People. Within these two gang nations, formal alliances have been struck, including rules, bylaws, and treaties.

Because distrust, estrangement, impoverishment, and social isolation typify many inner-city black communities, gangs, crime, and violence touch most households. The result is a process of *social catastrophe*. This prompts young people, who have insufficient social support at home—from neglectful, unemployed or underemployed, alienated, or absent parents—to fail in other environments, primarily in school. Social catastrophe drives these young people to the streets for answers and social support. Social catastrophe, of course, is not exclusive to inner-city black gangs. In the 1990s, black gangs gained a multigenerational presence within families.

Asian Gangs

During the 1970s, political upheavals prompted the immigration of more than one million Asian refugees to the United States. *Asian gangs*, which primarily include Cambodians, Laotians, and Vietnamese, generally comprise thirteen-to thirty-five year-olds. They are not as easy to distinguish as black and Hispanic gangs, because most Asian gangs choose not to identify themselves by color, clothing styles, and other gang symbols.

Asian gangs are particularly motivated by money and are notorious for victimizing members of their own ethnic group. Their crimes of choice include residential robberies, extortion, auto thefts, and gambling. Informal gangs often work a particular territory. Traveling gangs, which are highly mobile because they do not defend turf, easily move across state lines to commit their crimes.

White Gangs

Caucasian or *white gangs* began to form in the late 1980s. They started as individuals seeking protection from other gangs at school or in the neighborhoods.

Like minority gangs, white gangs are growing rapidly. Members, generally ranging in age from eleven to early twenties, increasingly come from disorganized or disrupted middle- or upper-middle-class families. Many no longer live at home and are considered *throwaways*. Gangs become a refuge and a resource. White gangs generally have better opportunities for integrating with their particular communities than blacks and Hispanics.

According to the California Department of Education (*On Alert! Gang Prevention*, 1994), white gangs fall into four basic categories: loners, funseekers or bashers, stoners, and skinheads.

Loners live in ethnic or multiethnic neighborhoods and belong to the gang in that neighborhood. They often come from transient and dysfunctional families. Long-term gang members do not trust them.

Fun-seekers or *bashers* are loosely organized groups. They conduct hate crimes against homosexuals and other ethnic and religious groups. They tend to live in urban and suburban areas.

Stoners are difficult to classify as gangs, though their activities are often violent and illegal. Stoners, who often indulge heavily in drugs, also frequently worship Satan. They are generally isolated and do not get involved in street violence.

Skinheads often portray strong physical identities—shaved heads, heavy, steel-toed boots, bomber jackets, and racist tattoos. *Racist skinheads* follow racist doctrines and frequently affiliate with adult white supremacist groups and/or the neo-Nazi movement. *Anarchist skinheads* have the same appearance as racist skinheads, however, they have a multiracial membership and believe that everyone is equal and should not be discriminated against because of skin color, religion, or heritage.

Suburban Gangs

Other youth gangs that have developed since the 1960s are the *suburban gangs*. I will describe them briefly, because they defy the stereotype that gangs exist only in the inner cities, where economic, educational, and social opportunities are largely absent. According to Dan Korem, in his book *Suburban Gangs: The Affluent Rebels* (1994), suburban gangs are often affluent gangs, defined by their activities. In addition, they have been studied in terms of the context of their criminal activities: delinquent, ideological, and occultic.

Affluent *delinquent gangs* desire profit and brutality. The lure of this kind of suburban gang is typically financial, physical or sexual assaults, and thrills. These most closely parallel inner-city gangs. They attract younger members—usually those in their early teens—and they seek to get their own way or what does not belong to them.

Ideological gangs attach themselves to a particular ideology, which may or may not be political, such as hate gangs. This kind of gang gives its members the opportunity to believe in a particular ideology, which, at least superficially, is a unifying factor. Participation in the gang feeds a distorted sense of self-worth. Hate gang members, such as skinheads, thrive on having power over others, and their gang activity gives them a chance to relieve stored-up anger.

Occultic gangs become attached to beliefs in occultic powers. These gang members focus on some occultic entity or practice, such as Satan or a Ouija board, to whom they pledge their ultimate allegiance in the hope that they can derive some kind of paranormal or supernatural powers from their involvement. Most occultic gang members are literate because of the need to read and retain extremely abstract thoughts. Their obsessively secretive nature prompts these gangs to be small in number—ten or fewer. They also tend to have more female than male members.

RISK FACTORS

Today, status continues to play a central role in gang membership. The status of the individual—or lack of it—often perpetuates the life of the youth gang. External threats and frustrations to this individual status include adult institutions, such as schools and jobs, community institutions, and the gang culture. There also are significant *risk factors* that make children vulnerable to the gang life.

Gang Profile: The Family

Certainly it would be advantageous to predict the likely profile of a youth gang member. If we were able to forecast which youths were most likely to be at risk for gang involvement, we could then initiate preventive measures to keep these youths from ever joining gangs. This would also help with intervention methods to disengage youths.

Many researchers have tried to discover what youth gang members have in common. The vast majority of members have come from a broken, an unstable, or a severely dysfunctional home. At least one of the following conditions is present in their home:

- Divorce or separation.
- Single-parent household, often with many siblings.
- Physical, verbal, emotional abuse/isolation, and/or sexual abuse. Note that in a 1998 study conducted by Weeks and Widom, in conjunction with the National Institute of Justice, sixty-eight percent of adult male felons at a New York State prison suffered physical abuse, sexual abuse, or neglect before age twelve.
- At least one dysfunctional parent, with problems involving, but not limited to, alcoholism, substance abuse, and bulimia.
- Poor family management, including minimal parental or guardian support or guidance, unclear or inconsistent rules for behavior, lax or nonexistent parental supervision, and high levels of interpersonal conflict or violence.
- People other than immediate family members living in the home.
- History of gang members in the family and/or gang members living in the same home, as well as parents or siblings who have a positive attitude toward gang membership.

These conditions produce a kind of pain that acts as a magnet for those who experience it. Coupled with this pain, many of these young people become more rebellious due to lack of parental involvement, including everything from love and support to restraint and discipline.

Adolescents will naturally test the limits within their own homes. This is how they practice emerging adulthood. Until the 1990s, rebelling teens might have stayed out past curfew or sneaked a beer. Today, however, many of these teens are getting involved in more extreme activities, with greater consequences. When youth gangs serve as the response to the voids in needy teens' lives, these surrogate families take control over the rebellious youths' activities, many of which are illegal.

It is important to make a distinction here. Yes, parents should share the responsibility for the level of intensity of the rebellion in a child's life. But youths are accountable for the rebellion itself. It is their choice how they will respond to circumstances in life. Therefore, teens' backgrounds cannot be used as an excuse to violate the law.

> ". . . someone with nothing to lose and angry with the world." *(Answar, 17, Inner City)*

> ". . . very dangerous and carrying a gun." *(Amber, 16, Inner City)*

> ". . . threatening, but more hype than reality." *(B.D., 16, Urban)*

> ". . . dangerous." *(Brandon, 16, Inner City)*

Other Factors

Many economic, social, and financial factors induce young people to join gangs. The child's own motivation is also important.

Gang-infested neighborhoods are typically found in economically depressed communities. Because families often reflect these existing economic conditions, they are often weak and fragmented. Some teens and younger youths seek a sense of family and safety outside of the home. One in four youths surveyed for this book turned to youth gangs for a "sense of family." Comparably, twenty-five percent of these youths also turned to their group to satisfy their own need for "refuge." Teens look to gangs—peers—to help them develop a sense of self-worth and importance, a sense of belonging, and a sense of guidance and nurturing.

Other neighborhood factors, according to a study by Hill, Howell, Hawkins, and Battin (1998), include the availability of marijuana, neighborhood youth in trouble, and low neighborhood attachment. Communities play a part too. Communities with a history of gang activity, with other undesirable elements that are generally accepted by gang members, are at risk for nurturing gangs. One-third of surveyed youths joined their gangs or groups because their friends were already involved.

Risk factors in the school are crucial as well. The Hill et al. study lists these factors: low academic aspirations, low school commitment, low school attachment, low academic achievement in elementary school, and an identified learning disability.

Individual response to youth gangs, of course, has the ultimate impact. Important factors, according to the youth survey, include:

- A teenager's existing rebelliousness and/or antisocial personality.

- An adolescent's pursuit of personal identity, pride, respect, and recognition, usually not available in the mainstream. Thirty-six percent of youths surveyed look to their gang or group to provide them with "status or identity."

- Deviant, delinquent, and often illegal behavior.

- Rejection of middle-class goals.

- Fear of exclusion. One in ten youths who contributed information to this book said that they had "no other choice" when selecting a particular group of friends.

- Violent behavior toward others, which often is founded in fear of physical harm to self or family.

- Cultural and language differences.

HIERARCHY OF MEMBERSHIP

Like any organization, youth gangs require structure to operate efficiently. From region to region, neighborhood to neighborhood, youth gangs operate distinctively. However, they have some common levels of membership, participation, and commitment.

Older members—often referred to as *OGs*, or *original gangsters*—have more extensive criminal backgrounds. They usually become the gang *leaders*. Because of their tenure and street smarts, they often use newer members to carry out their commands. To survive, OGs must be logical, streetwise, and mentally and physically tough. They also must be able to become violent instantaneously. Leadership in gangs is transitory. If they survive the gang life, they become *veteranos*—former gang members who are no longer active in the day-to-day activities.

"Most of the gang is crazy, and they do it for attention. Older gangsters do it more for the money and power." *(Paul, 15, Inner City)*

"They look for status, power, and money, and pick on the weak." *(Christopher, 18, Urban)*

Hard-cores are typically young adults in their late teens and early twenties. They are completely immersed in the gang culture, often to the exclusion of their own biological families. The gang is their family. They live by the gang rules, and they will die in defense of the gang. Hard-cores comprise up to fifteen percent of gang memberships.

"They'll do anything to get by or to pull status and feel wanted." *(Richard, 19, Urban)*

". . . a group of homies who would ride and die for each other." *(Answar, 17, Inner City)*

Regulars are those who participate in the gang's criminal and noncriminal activities on a consistent and frequent basis. Though they are younger—usually ages fourteen to twenty—they are members in good standing and back up the hard-cores in words—and actions. They often commit crimes for the older gang members.

". . . the younger members of the gang, from thirteen to nineteen, who do most of the fighting and shooting. They're 'YGs' until they earn their rank." *(Pete, 16, Inner City)*

Soldiers or *peons* are reliable, but low-status, gang members.

Recruits are usually younger, though sometimes older youths, who are recruited for specific skills or talents. They are often invited to join for a limited time.

Associates are youths who occasionally connect with the gang on the street or elsewhere. Ordinarily, they are not recognized or identified as gang members.

Peripherals include those who participate periodically and selectively in gang events. They do not usually have high status, nor are they regarded as being reliable or committed to the gang. They readily leave the gang and can be excused from many of the gang's activities.

Taggers—or graffiti artists—are often gangs unto themselves. These smaller groups, also known as *crews, cliques,* or *posses,* use the city as their canvas. They use spray paint, felt pens, and paintbrushes to vandalize public buildings. Taggers sometimes violate turf boundaries, which can prompt retaliation from traditional youth gangs.

Wanna-bes—averaging between ten and thirteen years old—are not official members of the gang, but they act as, or claim to be, part of the gang. They often dress in gang attire, spend time with gang members, create graffiti, and commit crimes to impress the gang.

> "... a kid who is still searching for an identity." *(Berra, 13, Urban)*

Potentials or *could-bes* live in or close to areas where there are active youth gangs, or they have a family member who is already a member of the gang. Potentials are not yet involved with the gang and can still freely choose other alternatives. Efforts to prevent a youth's gang involvement are most successful with this group.

> "Anyone could be a youth gang member, even the one that you least suspect." *(Kent, 15, Urban)*

Chapter Highlights

- Early American *gangs* divided themselves primarily along ethnic, racial, and cultural lines. Other defining factors were urbanization and poverty.
- Finding a specific definition for *gang* is difficult because of the diversity of groups the term has tried to include.
- It also is important to distinguish between gangs and groups. While teens form groups to be together and to belong to something, gangs represent extremes—often illegal ones—in these peer connections, expectations, and experiences.
- *Youth gangs* consist of adolescents and young adults who:
  —Interact frequently and share a common identity.
  —Express their identity through a name, language, and symbols unique to their gang.
  —Exercise territorialism—protect their turf.
  —Repeatedly engage in illegal activities.

—Have identifiable leadership.

—Participate in continuous association and interaction.

- Gangs originally formed in this country along ethnic and racial lines. Socioeconomic status also played a role.

- *Hispanic gangs* first developed as neighborhood groups in the 1900s. Decades later, they organized to protect themselves from outside influences, including criminals and law enforcement. Today, multigenerational involvement is not uncommon.

- *African-American* or *black gangs* began in the 1920s as nonviolent, loose associations.

- Black youths experience high levels of *social catastrophe* in which gangs, crime, and violence touch most inner-city households.

- During the 1970s, political upheavals prompted the immigration of more than one million Asian refugees to the United States. *Asian gangs* are more difficult to distinguish because they choose not to identify themselves by color, clothing, and other typical gang symbols.

- *Caucasian* or *white gangs* began to form in the late 1980s. They started as individuals seeking protection from other gangs at school or in the neighborhoods.

- White gangs fall into four basic categories: *loners, fun-seekers* or *bashers, stoners,* and *skinheads—racist* and *anarchist.*

- *Suburban gangs* defy the stereotype that gangs exist only in the inner city.

- Suburban gangs often are affluent gangs, defined by their activities: delinquency, ideology, and occultism.

- *Delinquent gangs* desire profit and brutality. *Ideological gangs* attach themselves to a particular ideology, which may or may not be political, such as hate gangs. *Occultic gangs* become attached to beliefs in occultic powers, such as Satan or a Ouija board.

- Several *risk factors* help distinguish the potential for a youth's joining a gang. Many of these originate in the family, especially in those families that are broken, unstable, or severely dysfunctional.

- Parents should share in the responsibility for the level of intensity of rebellion in their child. However, it is the child who is accountable for the rebellion itself.

- Gang-infested neighborhoods are typically found in economically depressed communities. These conditions often motivate the child to seek family stability outside of the biological family.

- Other risk factors influencing the child include, but are not limited to, community conditions, school, peers, and individual responses.

- Gangs have their own *hierarchy of membership*. Common to most are: *veteranos, original gangsters* (OGs) or *leaders, hard-cores, regulars, soldiers* or *peons, recruits, associates, peripherals, taggers, wanna-bes*, and *potentials* or *could-bes*.

Chapter 5

Gang Engagement

Not long ago, after school, my friends and I were walking home when a group of people came up to us and asked us if we wanted to be in what they called a gang. I looked at my friends and hoped they would decline, but one of my friends, Kayte, decided to "act cool" and joined. I was so happy that Lisa, my other friend, and I were responsible for our actions and walked away.

Kayte stayed to be "beat in," and I mean beat in. They beat her to see if she would be strong enough for their gang. That was the very last time I saw her happy before I saw something I regret seeing. I talked with her over the phone, hoping I could put some sense into her. She said she would be fine and that she would see me at school the next day. She never came. I thought she was probably robbing a store or jacking a car.

That night when I called her, there was no answer. I got worried and decided to take a walk. I don't know why, but I found myself headed down the street where she and I would go as little girls to jump rope. I was so relieved to look up and see her coming toward me. I walked a little faster, moving to the side, because of the speeding car in back of me. Then it happened. As the car rushed down the street, the passenger pulled out a gun, and, in an instant, shot my helpless friend in the head.

I couldn't believe it. I had just seen my best friend brutally murdered on the street that she and I had long ago played on. I ran to her side and hugged her, feeling her blood run onto my clothes. I wished so much that I could have saved her. I wanted to be able to turn back time and jump in front of that bullet to die for her. But, now, she has gone from my life forever, and there is nothing I can do about it. *(Renee, 14, Urban)*

GETTING INVOLVED

Every young person needs to feel a sense of self-worth, identity, acceptance, recognition, companionship, belonging, purpose, and security. Gangs, with their promises of adventure, danger, high risk, and a sense of the unknown, offer what traditional systems have failed to provide.

Personal Motivations

Youths join gangs for a variety of reasons. A list of justifications, offered by the California Department of Education through its 1994 publication *On Alert! Gang Prevention*, includes: fear, curiosity, excitement, prestige, peer pressure, lack of education, poor employment skills or unemployment, a family history of gang involvement, economic gain, and a lack of alternatives.

Personal motivations for joining gangs include, but are certainly not limited to, the following:

• Friendship, social bonding, shared experiences, tradition, and feelings of belonging (remember, these are the same reasons described in Chapter 2 for youths to join *any* group).
• Role models who take charge and protect their gang members, as well as set the rules and standards for gang behavior—a substitute for parents!
• A chance to succeed in the gang because of personal failures in traditional settings, especially school.
• Fun, thrills and excitement.
• A viable group alternative when all others have rejected them; a group of allies to "hang out with" and, often, "die for."
• Economic opportunities—often illegal—which provide personal resources and promote personal freedom.
• Protection and safety from traditional institutions and rival gangs.
• Status and prestige; including the need for recognition and reputation.

The Missing Protector Factor

What most youths are consciously or unconsciously seeking is a release from pain—the pain affiliated with dysfunctional family lives. These youths often seek help, and no one answers. When in crisis, needy youths turn to family members—hopefully adults—for aid, and no one is home. Thus, this *Missing Protector Factor* sends them out, anywhere, to find support and comfort. Youths look to their gangs to help mask their pain, provide distractions for that pain, and provide them with empowerment over their pain. In their gangs, these injured youths are seeking some kind of stability, even permanence, to help them through their turmoil. They seek cohesion, not isolation. This is more than just a desire to belong to a group!

RECRUITMENT

In many communities, joining a gang is considered a desirable, honorable, and expected commitment. Joining a gang is never solely the joiner's decision, however. The gang itself both recruits and initiates the membership, as well as protects and perpetuates the stability of the gang structure. Twenty-seven percent of the youth survey participants said they were "recruited" into their current group of friends.

The Push-Pull of Membership

Joining a youth gang is often the result of combined approaches: push and pull. The *pull*—or that which attracts the person to join—often involves four primary attractions: the lure of money, the sense of family, the assurance of protection, and the enticement of family. Of course, these attractions also serve as a *push*—an external force compelling gang membership.

Today, the primary reason for a push-pull is the perceived need for protection, especially in gang-saturated neighborhoods:

"I stayed in the same hood with a gang, and they wanted me to ride with them. I needed the protection." *(Answar, 17, Inner City)*

"I wanted to have protection from other people and wanted to fit in." *(Tina, 17, Suburban)*

The word "perception," as it relates to protection, is important here, because national research conducted by the National Institute of Justice in 1998 indicates a different reality. In *Comparing the Criminal Behavior of Gang Members and At-Risk Youths*, C. Ronald Huff explains that youths can resist overtures to join a gang without serious reprisals. According to Huff, and contrary to popular belief, the majority of respondents who knew individuals who had refused to join a gang reported that those individuals suffered no consequences for their refusal. And, for those youths who did resist—and experienced consequences—the consequences were often milder than the serious assaults endured by youths during the initiation into the gang. Most important, youths who resist gangs are less likely to experience the arrest, incarceration, injury, and death associated with gang membership.

Still, many will succumb to the push-pull pressures of gang recruitment. Gangs can provide immediate gratification to an economically disadvantaged youth, or one who has been forgotten—especially one who has been excluded, or not yet included. This makes young children in school environments particularly vulnerable targets, because schools idealistically represent healthy social interactions. When a child is not part of that process, he or she will look elsewhere for acceptance, or that child will be "marked" by a gang for potential recruitment. At-risk youths often identify with the nearest "friend," regardless of how negative that attraction proves to be.

> "All the boys I grew up with in my neighborhood were in a gang." *(D.G., 16, Urban)*

> "I was born and raised in a gang." *(Stevie, 15, Inner City)*

> "My family was already out of the gang. They used to tell me that I shouldn't join. I thought they were trying to tell me that I wasn't tough enough. I joined to fit in with my family." *(Pete, 16, Inner City)*

> "Brotherhood. I've got a big brother, but we're more like strangers. We never communicated. So I took it upon myself to replace him!" *(Zannie, 17, Inner City)*

> "I joined to make money and fight other gangs. . . . Just for fun." *(Joseph, 17, Inner City)*

"My family was involved with my gang, and I wanted to go down for them and my gang. I got status by doing crazy things like drive-by shootings." *(Moniqua, 16, Inner City)*

"I joined because they were my uncles. I looked up to them because my father was never around." *(Jack, 16, Inner City)*

"My family trained me to do the things required in the gang." *(Darren, 17, Urban)*

"I didn't feel cared for by my family." *(Ricky, 18, Inner City)*

"I felt the need to belong to people, and I felt found in the gang. But I was wrong!" *(Natasha, 16, Suburban)*

Power and Status

Power through status—this is a primary motivation for gang membership. From their affiliation with gangs, youths acquire a sense of identity and status from being a member. This sets them apart from their classmates and families. Being a gang member is particularly important to those who cannot or do not succeed in other, more legitimate activities, such as school, sports, or employment. Thirty-six percent of the youths surveyed looked to their group to satisfy their need for "status."

". . . to build a reputation and to become someone of a higher 'power'!" *(Richard, 19, Urban)*

"The gang makes me feel good, and I like to fight other gang members. It's all about power and control." *(Wayne, 15, Urban)*

Membership, however, presents constant struggles to gain status. Often, violent behavior is used to create and sustain status. This need for status also creates internal competitions that impact the hierarchy of the gang. Thus, leadership—and often the very formation of the gang—is always in flux.

ENTRY

Typically, the process of joining a gang is gradual. It usually evolves, often taking a year or more to come to fruition. Violence is a hallmark activity for gangs and helps them strengthen their bonds between existing members and between the new recruits. The use of violence also increases the stake of prospective or fringe members.

Initiations and Violence

A ritual. A rite of passage. A coming of age. A violent experience . . . the gang initiation. This initiation ritual satisfies several functions:

- To determine whether a potential gang member is tough enough to endure the rigors of violence he or she will certainly face.
- To increase solidarity among gang members by engaging them in a collective ritual.
- To communicate information about the gang, its rules, and its activities.

Incoming gang members often go through this ritual of violence by being beaten up by existing members. Or, they might drink alcohol or take drugs. This is called being "beat in" or "v'ed in" or "jumped in" or "turning" or "courted." The name and details of the initiation process will vary, depending on where the youth gang is located.

> "I was beat up and . . . wanted it. I really wanted to impress my brother and his friends." *(Raymond, 17, Urban)*

In many gang communities, initiates have a choice between the ritual and a "mission." A mission requires the incoming member to participate in, or initiate, some form of illegal behavior—usually an act of violence—and often against a rival gang on rival turf.

The use of violence in the initiation process is important for several reasons. Violence, and its ever-present threat, is a constant in gang life. Violence communicates a message to gang members and non-gang members. The message? "This is the life we live—a violent one—and we are not afraid to use it or receive it!"

Violence also reinforces solidarity within the group, especially when it relates to the gang's dealings with other gangs and the outside world.

Females in Gangs

Females have traditionally been perceived as secondary to males in the development of youth gangs. This has been changing, and today, up to thirty percent of gang membership is female. In relation to males, females can also be equally, and often more, violent than their male counterparts.

> "I was affiliated with the gang because my brother, my cousin, and my boyfriend were dons in the gang. I liked the power, theirs and mine." *(Shaney, 16, Inner City)*

Generally, females join because they choose to do so. By hanging out with gang members, they get a sampling of the life and attach themselves to the gang.

> "I had no parents, and I wanted to be part of a family. This was the best way I could find. Plus, my cousin Steven was killed by a rival gang, and this was a way of getting revenge. My mom is in the same rival gang, and my joining was a way to get back at her too." *(Selena, 15, Suburban)*

Female initiations often require young girls and young women to participate in sexual acts with gang members or demonstrate "courage" by committing illegal acts. This is particularly significant for females, because most female gang members already experience vulnerabilities with their self-achievement, self-esteem, and self-worth. A substantial number of female gang members have been the victims of abuse.

> "I know a lot of people in gangs are real bad, but for a teen to get involved in the first place means something is not right in that girl's life. Somehow she is hurt and doesn't know how to fix the way she feels. Once she falls into a gang, she falls all the way in." *(Elia, 17, Inner City)*

While females do get involved in violent crimes, they tend to commit the greater proportion of status offenses, such as becoming runaways.

> "I was a runaway, and I needed acceptance, a place to stay, and to be loved." *(Cassandra, 15, Inner City)*

Often, female gang members use their affiliation with a gang to shock their families and others who did not accept them before.

> "I really don't know why I joined. I thought I knew it was the right decision, but I guess it was the wrong one." *(Elizabeth, 16, Inner City)*

Male gang members often do not trust females to protect group secrets, so the females are frequently excluded from the planning and performance of crimes. However, in the 1990s, females agitated for increased equality. They started to look for approval, not only from the gang's male membership but from the other females as well. In rebellion or by preference, some form their own female gangs.

Choosing Not to Join a Gang

I would be remiss if I did not include survey responses from youths across the country who decided *not* to join a youth gang.

> "I was dependent on myself. I had to take care of my own needs. I played it smart and realized that a gang was trouble. I wanted to live and survive to live life another way." *(Christopher, 18, Urban)*

> "My parents told me gangs are bad news and to stay away from them." *(Kent, 15, Urban)*

> "My family and I didn't want my little brothers or sisters to join." *(Nikki, 17, Suburban)*

> ". . . lame and pointless. Why get beat up to hang out?" *(Marie, 16, Inner City)*

> "I never met any gang members until I was locked up, and I didn't like any of them. So, I'm anti-gang." *(Ray, 17, Urban)*

> "I've *never* had the opportunity or desire. The values of gang members—violence, materialism, coercion, illegal activities (like drug use and sales)—have *never* appealed to me." *(Olivia, 21, Urban)*

"I didn't join a gang after I saw them always running. They would run from police, from problems, from rivals. . . . That is no way to live, and things don't get fixed by running. They always seem to run faster than the person running away." *(Danna, 17, Urban)*

"I knew it would break my mother's heart. I am the oldest of five girls, and they look up to me." *(Laquitta, 17, Urban)*

"I was never approached by a gang. If I had been approached, though, I would refuse to join, because I don't like putting my life on the line for someone who may end up killing me one day." *(Jake, 16, Rural)*

Chapter Highlights

- Youth gangs—with their promises of adventure, danger, high risk, and a sense of the unknown—offer what traditional systems have failed to provide.
- *Personal motivations* for joining a gang are many. Just a few include:
  —Protection and safety.
  —Friendship, belonging, shared experiences, tradition, and social bonding.
  —Role models who take care of them.
  —A chance to succeed in a gang.
  —Fun, thrills, and excitement.
  —A viable group alternative.
  —Economic opportunities.
  —Status and prestige.
- When children need adult help in a crisis, and no one is home—the *Missing Protector Factor*—they turn elsewhere for support, often to the streets.
- In many communities, joining a gang is considered a desirable, honorable, and expected commitment.
- Joining a gang is often the result of combined approaches: push and pull. The *pull* attracts the person to join, including the primary attractions of the lure of money, the sense of family, the assurance of protection, and the enticement of family. The *push* is an external force that compels gang membership. Often, the push and the pull are the same motivators.

- Power through status is a primary motivation for gang membership.
- Typically, the process of joining a youth gang is gradual and often takes a year or more.
- The gang initiation, generally quite violent, satisfies several needs, including:

  —Determining how well the potential member will endure the rigors of gang violence.

  —Increasing solidarity among gang members.

  —Communicating information about the gang, its rules, and its activities.
- Females have traditionally taken on a secondary role in the gang. Today, however, up to thirty percent of gang membership is female.
- Female initiations often require young girls and young women to participate in sexual acts with gang members or demonstrate "courage" by committing illegal acts.
- Often, female gang members use their gang affiliation to shock their families and friends.

Chapter 6

Scope of Influence

People now walk down the street,
During the day or night,
In fear of being beat
Or getting in a fight.

Kids nowadays are being taught
Not to talk to any stranger.
For, if they do and are caught,
Their lives may be in danger.

T.S., 15, Urban

GANG CULTURE

Understanding the gang requires understanding the gang culture. This might include symbols, values, and traditions unique to that gang, which help form the distinctive identity of the gang and its members.

Development

Gangs arise when traditional, established institutions fail to meet the needs, resolve the issues, or include the participation of particular youths.

Each local community provides a different context for the development of youth gangs. Influencing this development are racial, ethnic, cultural, and socioeconomic conditions in that community and its neighborhoods.

The *clique* serves as a basic building block for the gang. It is a relatively cohesive subunit that frequently provides the gang with its distinctiveness and consistency. Cliques often carry out functions for the gang that are best pursued by a smaller unit. Because they are small, they also have the advantage of being more fluid and flexible than the larger group.

Youth gangs often organize themselves around a particular territory or turf. This readily helps them craft their gang identity and creates the foundation for their attitudes and behaviors. Thirty-nine percent of the youths surveyed said that gangs in their communities were "protective"; twenty-seven percent considered them a "unifying force." Thirty-seven percent said gangs in their neighborhoods are "ever-present."

> "Looking at people in my neighborhood and my family . . . the gang represents everything about where I came from, and where I'm going." *(Robert, 16, Inner City)*

> "All my friends were in the gang, so I got in it." *(Bob, 17, Suburban)*

Of course, the level of commitment to territorialism is influenced by cultural traditions, community stability, socioeconomic variables, the age of gang members, the evolving interests of the gang, and the degree of mobility for gang members.

As the economic involvement of gangs grows and produces prosperity—through drug trafficking and other illegal activities—gangs take on a more entrepreneurial, corporate, or business structure.

> "I joined to get more drugs, money, cars, and protection." *(Keith, 15, Inner City)*

> "I liked the lifestyle." *(Stephen, 16, Inner City)*

Values

In the absence of formal rules, sanctions, and lines of authority to direct the members, *values* help identify goals and shape behavior. In the absence of formal rules, sanctions, and lines of authority to direct the members, values help identify goals and shape behavior. Gang members define their values as something that holds them together and gives them individual and collective purpose and identity. Each gang's value system represents a particular standard of behavior and code of survival. Shared values help youth gang members understand the expectations they have of each other and establish the limits for individual thoughts and actions.

Values—through outward symbols and behaviors—transmit messages about gang identity to allies, rivals, and strangers. These symbols also unify the members through the special meanings they hold for each particular gang.

One significant influence in the development of gang values and the transmission of symbols is *popular culture*. Through popular culture—movies, music videos, audio recordings, television, computers, radios, and other media—gang symbols are transmitted. This helps explain why similar behaviors, attitudes, symbols, and values can spring up simultaneously on different continents.

The age, ethnicity, and socioeconomic status of members also influence the values of the gang. Because they have been excluded from—or not yet included in—mainstream society, the members look to their gangs to fill this gap.

Gang members seek a foundation and values that the mainstream has left out of their reach. Like other young people, they are taught to believe in the American Dream. Gang members desire cars, clothes, electronic equipment, and success—however measured. They expect the same economic success and material achievements as other young people. Yet they have become outsiders, and they are often deprived of the legitimate tools—through education and employment—to reach and experience this ultimate lifestyle. When they perceive that they cannot achieve their goals legitimately, the gang—as a responsive counter—helps its members attain "the dream" illegitimately, illegally. Often, these youths have the same social expectations, but they are forced to achieve them through different, often illegal, means.

> "When you have about fifteen to twenty homies, and all of you are on the same page about making money, you should help each other out. In the long run, it either pays off or it doesn't. It's no different than any other enterprise." *(D.S., 16, Suburban)*

Youth gang involvement has helped members anticipate their futures favorably. They believe that gang participation has outfitted them with the insights and skills to improve the conditions of their lives.

DRUGS AND OTHER CRIMINAL ACTIVITIES

For many members, affiliation with their youth gang has served them with the "training" to survive in and surpass a society that offers them few opportunities for developing their individual talents. Much of this training is founded in crime.

The Business of Trafficking

Similar to other business organizations, the gang's survival depends on its ability to develop and maintain a sound financial base. This requires money to buy weapons, to transact for drugs, to bail members out of jail, to pay attorney's fees, and to have parties. To accommodate these needs, youth gangs have been spirited into illegal activities, especially drug trafficking.

The changing labor market conditions of the 1960s and 1970s, especially the reduced employment of low-skilled manufacturing jobs, made it difficult for older gang members to find legitimate jobs. In addition, the increasing demand for drugs, especially cocaine, gave rise to economic advantages to the gang. This was aided by the spiraling popularity of drug use in the United States and the burgeoning international cocaine trade.

By the middle of the 1980s, across the country youth gang members themselves were heavy drug users, but not yet traffickers. Economic survival—and the illegal drug economy—created pressures to grow youth gangs as the economic foundation for drug trafficking, often for organized crime. Note, though, that the profits from drug sales often do not get back to the gang. Rather, a member's earnings frequently accumulate only to the seller, who might spend the money on typical teen purchases such as clothes, entertainment, jewelry, or on more drugs to resell. Ironically, most youths do not join their gangs to sell drugs; however, once in the gang, this opportunity to make money takes on a greater importance.

Trafficking: Organization and Territory

From the outset, it is important to understand that all youth gang members do not sell or use drugs. In most youth gangs, however, members work their way up by starting as *runners* or *mules* for distributors within the gang. These younger members make deliveries of illegal drugs to customers. Even younger children, as young as age five, serve gangs as *scouts* for drug deals: they watch for law enforcement and warn the gang members of their approach during drug deals.

Street-level dealing is the job into which runners move. Most less experienced dealers become *hired dealers* and work for the distributor on consignment: as they sell the drugs, they pay the distributor. *Independent dealers* work for themselves.

Membership in the gang helps establish and maintain a drug-trafficking territory or turf. Once the turf is established, the dealer must find customers who will both buy the drugs and refer the dealer to other potential customers.

Juvenile Delinquency

Delinquency is not inborn, nor does it come along naturally. Children learn to become delinquents by becoming members of groups in which delinquent conduct is already the norm. It is "the thing to do."

Juvenile delinquency serves as a subculture, complete with knowledge, beliefs, values, codes, prejudices, and other factors that a youth absorbs through participation in a delinquent group.

Often, middle-class delinquents blame their parents, and other sources of authority, for everything that is wrong with their lives and their values. They, like lower-class delinquents, focus their energies on the middle and upper classes as targets for their disgust and delinquent behavior. Middle-class delinquency can often be a one-time experience.

Lower-class delinquents consider themselves rejected and oppressed by the middle class. They want to violate others for material gain or to reconcile a debt they believe society owes them.

Much of what both levels of delinquents steal, damage, or destroy has an intrinsic worth. For some, it is the object itself that produces the personal reward for the juvenile delinquent. For others, there is a level of enjoyment in the discomfort and loss that this delinquent act creates for others. Many delight in the defiance of the rules and the acquisition of status for this defiance. For most of these delinquents, the youth gang gives them a counterculture structure within which to find acceptance and direction in their delinquent behavior. The gang serves as a separate, distinct, and appealing focus of attraction, loyalty, and solidarity.

Certainly not all delinquents join youth gangs. However, according to most research, adolescents who join youth gangs are more involved in delinquent acts than are adolescents who do not join such gangs. Interestingly, though, it is difficult to determine the proportion of total crimes that can be attributed to youth gang members.

VIOLENCE

Violence is central to gang life. It is part of the everyday life in the gang, and it is excessively high in gang-infested neighborhoods and families. Forty-six percent of the youths surveyed for this book believe that gangs are "violent and destructive." Such violence finds its place in the very nature of gangs, from initiation to maintaining status as gang members to disengagement from the gang.

Why Violence?

Why is the level of violence so high among gang members? First, gangs are organized for violence. They provide training, weaponry, motives, discipline, and leadership for engaging in violence.

Another theory is that gangs magnify violence and provide a collective process to weaken the same social institutions that have rejected their members. Still a third explanation is that individuals are selected for membership based on their propensity for violence. Violence is the primary bond they share. For some, violence promotes the presumption of power.

> "It feels good, because then we know we have power." *(Wayne, 15, Urban)*

> "Sometimes being in the gang is needed to protect yourself from looking weak." *(Cassandra, 15, Inner City)*

> "People have always struggled for power. Violence is a part of everyday life . . . animal instinct. No matter how hard we try to suppress it, violence won't go away." *(Mathew, 17, Urban)*

> "Violence is effective, but will the people love you or fear you?" *(Beth, 15, Urban)*

> "Violence is a way of respect. If someone disrespects you, you resort to violence to let them know who has the power." *(George, 15, Inner City)*

For others, violence is ineffective and unnecessary. Forty percent of the youths surveyed asserted that youth gang influences in their communities are "more hype than reality." One in four said that these gangs are "insignificant."

". . . just a way of wanting attention." *(Khonemany, 17, Urban)*

". . . a sissy way of getting people to listen to you." *(Danna, 17, Urban)*

". . . a cowardly way to force someone to do something." *(David, 16, Suburban)*

"It shows the power of one using violence and the *willpower* of those being violated." *(Jantu, 14, Inner City)*

"Weak people use violence to solve things or get power over others." *(C.M., 17, Inner City)*

"Violence works, but it's not cool." *(Lynn, 20, Rural)*

". . . wrong and a sign of insecurity." *(Marisela, 16, Rural)*

". . . stupid, immature. . . . Violence usually starts at home." *(Selena, 15, Suburban)*

"Never try to gain power over others, because it causes corruption." *(Frank, 17, Suburban)*

"With violence you actually lose power . . . real power." *(Anthony, 17, Inner City)*

Violence comes in many forms. Some of it is functional, like gang members protecting their turf and homes and defending themselves from outsiders. Other forms of violence are expressive and represent symbolic threats to the gang and its members. Whatever the purpose of the violence, it generally leads to retaliation and revenge, which help perpetuate the cycle of violence in their neighborhoods.

"History shows us that violence is only a temporary means and, overall, causes further violence." *(Frank, 17, Suburban)*

"No violence is necessary unless other gangs retaliate and want to cease your existence." *(D.S., 16, Suburban)*

"You can't resolve anything with violence. All you do is create a more hostile situation." *(Nereyda, 17, Urban)*

The Threat

So what is *threat?* According to Scott H. Decker and Barrik Van Winkle in their book *Life in the Gang: Family, Friends, and Violence* (1996), threat describes a process in which perceptions and interactions work together to produce behavior. This process does not occur in a vacuum but takes place in a context influenced by the labor market, political forces, and other neighborhood opportunity structures. These structural forces produce external restraints that limit options and opportunities.

Most inner-city youths do not become gang members. However, the *perception of threat* in a gang area is real. Therefore, youths who are more affected than others often join gangs for protection against these threats of violence, especially from rival gangs. In fact, forty percent of youths surveyed described gang presence in their neighborhoods as "threatening." Thirty-seven percent depicted gangs in their communities as "fear-provoking."

The levels of threat and the violence itself will vary from neighborhood to neighborhood. It is important to weigh something else in evaluating these conditions. First, many people overestimate the level of gang violence, because they rely on media accounts, which often disproportionately report gang activities within the context of all news. Also, gang members themselves—bent on status and attention—often overstate levels of gang violence to elevate their own self-esteem. Gang members frequently talk violence more than they do it.

Chapter Highlights

- Gangs arise when traditional, established institutions fail to meet the needs, resolve the issues, or include the participation of particular youths.
- The *clique* serves as a basic building block for the gang.
- In the absence of formal rules, sanctions, or lines of authority to direct the members, *values* help identify goals and shape behavior.
- *Popular culture*—movies, music videos, audio recordings, television, com-

puters, radios, and other media—helps transmit gang symbols nationally and internationally.

- Like other young people, gang members are taught to believe in the American Dream. However, they have become outsiders, and they are often deprived of the legitimate tools—through education and employment—to reach and experience this ultimate lifestyle. Many, therefore, turn to illegal alternatives.
- Youth gangs provide their members with "training"—much of it founded in crime—to survive in and surpass society.
- Responding to market demands for illegal drugs in the 1960s and 1970s, youth gangs entered the world of enterprise through drug trafficking.
- Levels of involvement in street drug sales include *scout, runner* or *mole, hired dealers,* and *independent dealers.*
- *Juvenile delinquency* serves as a subculture for youths who participate in a delinquent group.
- Juvenile delinquency primarily involves middle- and lower-class youths.
- Violence is central to gang life—on a macro scale involving neighborhoods and a micro scale involving each member.
- Gangs are organized for violence: they create it, they magnify it, and they perpetuate it.
- The *threat* of violence describes a process in which perceptions and interactions work together to produce behavior.
- Most inner-city youths do *not* become gang members. Many who join gangs do so seeking protection from threats of violence, especially from rival gangs.

Chapter 7

Leaving the Gang

Courage is choosing to face the inevitable. To learn to go on when it seems as if everything is going wrong around you. To wake up in the morning with a smile, knowing in the back of your mind that each day is painstakingly harder. When the pain, hard work, grief, and suffering have piled on you like books in a library, you hold your head up high and go on living.

When you get a phone call saying that someone has passed on, your heart stops beating. You feel as though you, too, have died. When the heartache is unbearable, you stay strong and face the loss, understanding that death is a part of life and accept it. That is courage.

When you wake up knowing that you have no job, no money, and almost no home, all you set your mind on is supporting your family. When you don't anticipate how long and hard the day ahead of you will be . . . when you choose to get up and try to start your life over, knowing that there are no guarantees, just chances . . . when you think about others instead of yourself . . . that is courage. *(Cremson, 15, Suburban)*

As I sit by myself
I think of my life.
Through so many years, I've strived.
Striving for my knowledge and abilities,
I never knew it was always within me.

As I look upon the world,
I see its lack of responsibilities.
The young ones growing up,
Not knowing the meaning of honesty.

As they run wild on the filthy streets,
I know that soon their senses shall meet.
Trustworthy, this they shall learn.
Their senses of doubt will slowly burn.

As they see the light,
The darkness fades,
And their world will be bright.

No longer will they walk
The filthy streets.
Fears of the past
With their courage they shall defeat.

I look at my past and see
Everything that I have said
Has happened to me.

                                        Leslie, 13, Suburban

WHY YOUTHS LEAVE GANGS

Once most youths join a gang, it is extremely difficult to convince them to disengage. The reasons for leaving the gang are as diverse as the people who try to do it.

Maturing Out

Little research exists to explain why a particular youth leaves a particular gang at a particular time. Most studies suggest that gang members often *mature out*—gradually breaking away, growing away, from the gang life . . . from active gang member to revered *veterano*. At one time, this occurred by the time the member was in his or her late teens or early twenties. However, three primary factors now influence longer gang membership—sometimes extending involvement decades beyond adolescence:

1. Members, especially core members, do not move from their gang-infested neighborhoods. Through many kinds of pressure, including the

threat of violence, they continue to maintain close ties with other important members.

2. Gangs are producing greater economic incentives that encourage continued involvement.

3. Technology, in creating national gang networks and sophisticated member-tracking systems, is making disaffiliation more difficult.

Weighing Alternatives

For those youth gang members who do leave, more of them leave for positive reasons than for negative ones. This can occur when the exiting members realize the long-term negative consequences of gang membership, some of them life threatening.

Take note, however, that the success and permanence of a member's disengagement depend significantly on the gang's willingness to let the member quit. With this caveat in mind, several positive and negative reasons for disengagement follow:

- Youth members look for less traumatic alternatives to meet their social and economic needs.

- For many, the reality that the gang did not produce enough tangible benefits—and often exploited them—inspires them to leave.

- Violence, from initiation to disengagement, prompts many youth gang members to reconsider their affiliation. They are tired of the killing, the maiming, and the persistent fear of violence.

- A personal or physical crisis related to the gang can move a member to disavow the gang, at least involvement in violent gang activities. This might occur if the gang member suffered an injury during a gang fight, if the member killed a rival gang member, or if a family member died in a gang-related activity. All of this can also result in a religious conversion.

- The member wants to pursue a legitimate career opportunity or higher education. However, more and more, gangs expect their homeboys to create a coexistence between the new choice and their gang affiliation.

- When the gang leader is no better than an abusive parent, young members find little reason to stay in the gang.

- For those youths who value their gang membership because of other family involvement, that relative's disaffiliation can prompt their own.

- If a dysfunctional family prompted the youth's entry into the gang, any repair work that helps heal the family can help erase the child's reasons for being in the gang.

- Even when unable to resolve family issues, some youths learn how to address the damage inflicted by family turmoil. They learn how to cope with and redirect how they feel in a constructive rather than a destructive way.

- For some, incarceration is the only way to disengage. However, with the growth of gangs and gang influences in prison, this is becoming harder to accomplish.

- For females, exit opportunities often exist when they become pregnant, get married, go straight, become institutionalized, return to school, or take care of siblings. The predominant reason is pregnancy. After all, it would be difficult for the female member to serve two families: the gang and her own children.

- Some youths disengage from their gangs because the gangs themselves dissolve.

THE EXIT

In many gangs, the process of leaving the gang involves more violence than the initiation.

Exit Rituals

Whether it is called the *V-out* or being *jumped out* or *courted out* or something else, the *exit ritual* can be extremely violent. Even until the end, gangs use violence as an integral part of their activities.

For most gangs, violence is used during this ritual to discourage resignations. To reinforce this disincentive to resignation, these ceremonies are often life threatening. If this is not enough, gangs frequently threaten the exiting member's family, especially when they think the family is putting pressure on the resigning gang member to quit.

V-outs are also used to punish or kick out troublesome members. In addition, youth gangs use this ritual to make a statement about members who have not made a total commitment to the gang. This form of social control helps keep gang members in their place!

Avoiding the dangers and violence of the exit ritual will be difficult for those who want to quit the youth gang. Members of youth gangs who contributed to this book confirm that a violence-free exit might require youths and their families, quickly and quietly, to move out of the neighborhood, the city, or the state. Others suggested that exiting members make themselves totally unavailable to the gang by joining time-consuming activities, especially those involving sports or faith organizations, full-time employment outside the neighborhood, or full-time school attendance elsewhere. These choices are also available when the youth fades out of the gang.

Fading Out

Somewhat a hybrid of membership and disengagement is *fading out*. This gradual process involves many of the previously mentioned reasons for leaving, including marriage, family, and legal employment.

In fading out, gang members explain to their homeboys why they want to leave. It is up to the gang to accept or reject the request. Realistically, though, once the member is not wholeheartedly committed to gang life—and no longer available for its activities—the members are more likely to let the member out. It all comes down to one consideration: persons wanting out must decide to make themselves unavailable for gang activities. Again, how to handle this is up to the gang. Some will relieve the members; others will punish them.

> "I did join, but I later came to my senses and left the gang. Most people feel the same way, but think they can't leave. I'm proof they can." *(Raylene, 17, Inner City)*

For most members to fade out, family and community support are essential. The key to fading out is *intervention*. Gang members, especially younger ones, must be given activities and alternatives to help them fade out of the gang life. They need substantial, positive alternatives to justify their choice to leave. These exiting gang members can find support in this intervention process from many sources. For example, law enforcement has youth activity programs, like the Police Activities League, that offers alternative activities and group choices.

Social organizations, such as the United Way, and social service agencies, which are often connected with local government, offer a wide variety of activities, counseling, and support services for exiting youths and their families. Faith organizations also provide a full spectrum of youth and family support services and activities. Also, with schools now being recognized as one of the safest environments for children, administrators and teachers are taking the lead with intervention to help youths find alternatives to the gang life. Even local businesses are getting involved by sponsoring activities and providing employment opportunities.

Certainly, not to be forgotten because of its critical impact on the youth is the family. This is one of the most important involvement groups in intervention. The gang youth's family—if it can be a positive influence in the teen's life—must be involved in all the suggested avenues for intervention. For the youth to succeed in changing his or her friendship choices and behavior, the family must serve as a constant and consistent support system.

When asked how they would help a friend leave the gang, survey participants shared diverse opinions.

> "The decision to get out of a gang must be determined by the person who is thinking about getting out. My job is to remain a good role model and try to encourage my friend to change her life." *(Marisela, 16, Rural)*

> "Care about them. Get them involved and keep them busy with other things that help them. Talk to them about their involvement, and find out why they joined in the first place." *(Sarah, 17, Suburban)*

> "Talk to them and their parents about getting them to leave the gang voluntarily. The only way to get someone out of a gang is to show them that they are needed and loved . . . to show them that the gang is bad for them." *(Chanel, 16, Suburban)*

> "Pair him with someone who was in a gang who can talk to him about how he wasn't able to live a free life." *(Maria, 15, Urban)*

> "I would do positive things with my friend that will give him a rush." *(Kristina, 17, Urban)*

> "Talk to her. Tell her parents. Try to get help from a hotline. Take her to events that encourage youths to avoid gangs." *(Beth, 15, Urban)*

"I would make myself available to my friend. This way she would spend more time with me and less with the gang." *(Tonya, 17, Rural)*

"Send my friend to another state, away from bad places." *(Bill, 16, Inner City)*

"Leaving a gang is not easy, and the gang usually doesn't allow it. By myself, I couldn't get my friend out without the help of parents, the police, and the community." *(Serena, 17, Urban)*

Chapter Highlights

- The main reason for leaving a youth gang is *maturing out*—gradually breaking away, growing away, from the youth gang.
- Youths who leave youth gangs do so for a variety of reasons:
  —Less traumatic alternatives to meet their social and economic needs.
  —Desire for less exploitive group relationships.
  —Need to get away from violence.
  —Personal or physical crisis related to the gang.
  —Religious conversion.
  —Pursuit of legitimate career or educational opportunities.
  —Realization that the gang leader is no better than an abusive parent.
  —Healing in the biological family that makes a return feasible.
  —Ability to resolve personal crises.
  —Departure of relatives in a gang who originally inspired the membership.
  —Incarceration.
  —For females, pregnancy, marriage, straight living, being institutionalized, or school.
  —Dissolution of the gang itself.
- In many youth gangs, the process of leaving the gang involves more violence than the initiation. This violence is often used to discourage the departure of exiting members.
- *Fading out* is a gradual process that allows gang members to explain and demonstrate why they want to quit.

- Persons who want to quit their gangs must make themselves unavailable for gang activities.
- For younger members to fade out, family and community support are essential. The key is *intervention*.

Part III

Winning the War
Through Collaboration

Chapter 8

Total Community Commitment

I am alien to my society.
I can feel evil run through my veins.
Yet, I fight to control my anxiety.
To gain dominion of the life that has not been slain.

Constantly fighting to do the right thing,
I don't know how much longer I can stand.
To gain knowledge, to get up in front of everyone and sing,
I must find out just who I am.

Jennifer, 18, Urban

HISTORICAL PERSPECTIVE

To understand what it will take to resolve today's youth gang problems, it is essential for us to understand what efforts we have utilized up to this point.

Throughout the recent decades, four basic strategies for addressing youth gangs have emerged. According to Irving A. Spergel, in *The Youth Gang Problem: A Community Approach* (1995), these four strategies, in historic order, are:

1. Local community organization and mobilization.

2. Social intervention and youth outreach.

3. Providing social and economic opportunities.

4. Suppression (including formal and informal methods of social control and incarceration).

A fifth approach—organizational or institutional change and development—modifies and elaborates on the first four strategies.

Local Community Organization and Mobilization

The idea of organizing the local community was the first historic effort to respond to delinquent groups. Prior to World War II, local groups took on the organized responsibility of working within neighborhoods to avert youth gangs. Their efforts were focused on restoring a sense of local community through citizen involvement, support, and controls. All of this was devised to lead youths to more traditional and acceptable behavior.

As more blacks and Hispanics arrived in urban centers in the 1940s and 1950s, the coordination of these local pride efforts became more complex. Cultural diversity made things more complicated.

In the 1950s and 1960s, federal dollars were targeted to deal with racial issues, poverty, inner-city youths, and delinquency. The civil rights movement stimulated most community-based programs. As problems became more complex in the 1960s and 1970s, local community organizations had to stretch their resources and focus beyond that of delinquent or youth gangs. They had to expand their efforts to embrace housing, education, jobs, and citizen empowerment.

Philosophies changed in the 1970s and 1980s, when community mobilization shifted to the interests of the "good" local citizens versus the "bad." The individualized approach virtually disappeared. Rather than focusing on the youth gang member, or youth criminal, communities narrowed their efforts to address only the criminal event.

In the 1990s, community mobilization began to incorporate the development of coalitions of justice agencies. These included schools, community groups, and even former gang members, who work with local, state, and federal agencies and resources to address the problem of gangs and their violent and illegal activities.

Social Intervention and Youth Outreach

The 1950s produced a movement toward outreach services for deviant youths. Youth agency programs assumed that youth gangs could be redirected to fit the expectations and needs of the larger society. With the help of special programs such as peer mentoring, street gang programs, and group development activities, youths could be saved. These programs nearly disappeared by the 1960s and 1970s, due to the complex growth of gangs. At the same time, youth agencies started to pay attention to other forms of youth deviancy, such as status offenses, like runaways.

New interest in the youth gang problem emerged in the 1980s. Youth agencies and schools targeted younger youths, particularly *at-risk youths*—those who have been identified, because of social, economic, geographical, and other reasons, to be susceptible to negative behaviors and development. The refined mission was expanded to include the prevention of serious gang violence and criminal behavior. Today's gang-prevention and -intervention programs now include, but are not limited to:

- Crisis intervention—helping youths resolve their crises in the earliest stages.

- Outreach—making accessible to troubled youths a variety of organizations, programs, and individuals that can provide invaluable assistance and support.

- Diversion—directing youths away from getting involved with negative activities and groups by providing positive alternatives.

- Counseling—helping youths resolve their problems and personal issues.

- Role modeling—providing peers and adults with positive attitudes and behaviors as human examples of strength, high self-esteem, and personal success.

- Mentoring—offering youths assistance and direction through their connection with an adult or peer who can provide positive role modeling.

- Drug prevention and treatment—making available the education, programs, treatment, and human assistance to youths who need help in avoiding or kicking substance dependencies.

- Tattoo removal—establishing medically supervised programs to help youth gang members rid themselves of their tattoos, which symbolize their gang identities.

- Conflict resolution—developing programs and training to help youths learn how to respond to their own issues through reason, not anger and violence.

- Leadership development—involving youths in alternative programs to help them route their energies and talents toward positive leadership of themselves and others, rather than gang followership.

- Job training—working within the community to establish partnerships to offer job training and career development as positive, legal alternatives to gang involvement.
- Referrals for services—providing access to social, medical, employment, housing, and other services that can help gang youths and their families secure their needs and find support.
- Temporary shelter—offering housing assistance to youths and their families.
- Religious conversion—getting involved with diverse faith organizations to offer spiritual alternatives to the gang life.

Providing Social and Economic Opportunities

Rising rates of delinquency, unemployment, and school failure in the 1950s and 1960s prompted foundations and federal agencies to get more involved. They provided funds to change social institutions and establish new types of school and training programs for these at-risk youth.

Unfortunately, these programs did not focus sharply enough on the youth gang problem. Instead, they had broader agendas to deal with a variety of social problems, most of which did not appeal to or involve gang members. Two such examples—Head Start (a program to help preschoolers grow the needed skills for starting school) and the Job Corps (a program that helped school dropouts and other troubled youths to get jobs)—were successful in general terms. They helped at-risk youths with socialization, academic development, and job training and retraining. However, it is not clear if these programs targeted actual or potential gang members.

Suppression

The 1970s and the 1980s swept in a mood of expanding conservatism. Decision makers viewed youth gangs as increasingly more dangerous, evil, and unaffected by community-based institutions and national policies. This resulted in a hard-line approach: arrest, prosecution, and removal from society. Therefore, law enforcement, prosecutors, and the courts took on a primary role in the community's response to youth gangs.

The clearest embodiment of gang suppression is in the programs developed by law enforcement. Research shows that the suppression strategy has led to more arrests, more convictions, and longer stays in prison for gang members. Of course, this has prompted state legislative involvement. One widespread legislative response: build more prisons.

Schools, which have suffered the proliferation of youth gangs, also have developed suppression programs, with security guards, metal detectors, gang-culture seminars, dress codes, anti-graffiti campaigns, and more.

PREVENTION

Keeping a youth from joining a gang is the best and most promising way to address the gang problem. *Prevention*, like anything else that affects the entire community, requires a total community commitment. Survey participants—nearly eighty percent—believed that more activities, programs, and youth centers would be the best prevention for youth involvement in gangs. One in three respondents recommended that community organizations "talk to the kids . . . get involved with them."

Key Principles

In 1993, the Office of Juvenile Justice and Delinquency Prevention (OJJDP) released its report "Serious, Violence, and Chronic Juvenile Offenders: A Comprehensive Strategy." The authors of the report, John J. Wilson and James C. "Buddy" Howell, listed several key principles for preventing and reducing at-risk behavior and delinquency:

- *Strengthen families.* Families must provide more guidance and discipline, instill values, and serve as their children's first and primary teachers.
- *Support core social institutions.* These include schools, churches, and other community-based organizations.
- *Promote prevention strategies that reduce the impact of risk factors.* These also need to enhance the influence of protective factors in the youths' lives.
- *Intervene* with youths as soon as delinquent behavior occurs.
- *Create a wide range of graduated sanctions.* These need to include accountability and a continuum of services to respond appropriately to the needs of each juvenile offender.
- *Identify and restrain* the small segment of serious, violent, and chronic juvenile offenders.

Gang Members' Input

Expert recommendations for prevention and intervention will make sense only if the gang members themselves believe in the proposed alternatives. In their book *Life in the Gang: Family, Friends, and Violence* (1996), Scott Decker and Barrik Van Winkle determined a consensus from gang members about how to prevent someone from joining a gang.

The majority of gang members said the best way to stop individuals from joining gangs was to talk with them about the *risks of membership*. One emphatic point is the violence that saturates the life of a gang member, though even this does not affect those who are strongly determined to join a gang.

Another preventive measure requires more effective *sanctions* for gang membership. Parents and caregivers have an important role here, because they are the first-line authority figures to watch and discipline their children. This option, of course, requires parents to have an ongoing commitment to supervise and monitor their children's activities.

A third recommendation is the need for *alternatives*, specifically sports and jobs. Because gangs themselves offer sports alternatives, however, jobs have a greater appeal as a preventive tool. Education is also a positive alternative.

> "Offer programs that encourage them to talk to ex-gang members. Offer new alternatives." *(Maria, 15, Urban)*

> "Have more programs that involve people who have been there and can tell kids how they will end up if they keep getting in trouble." *(Bill, 16, Inner City)*

> "Offer positive things—things that are not gang-related—for gang members to do. Choices that are legal." *(Quinton, 15, Suburban)*

INTERVENTION

Ideally, gang prevention efforts will divert at-risk youths from joining gangs. Many experts believe that once a youth is involved with a gang, the chances for disengagement are highly reduced.

One-on-One Intervention

There are youths involved in gangs, however, who need help now. For these youths, a direct *one-on-one intervention* has the best chance for success. One-on-one intervention requires an appropriate connection between—and resolution of—the contributing familial problems, the promises of the gang to resolve those issues, and the most likely reasons for disengagement.

These factors must be matched for each youth. Stereotyping will not work. The purpose is to identify specifically what will induce a particular youth to disengage, considering the individual reasons for his or her gang involvement and the payoff(s) that gang membership has ensured. Then offer a substitute that provides the member with a greater promise or incentive than gang membership.

For example, a youth who joins a gang because of abuse in his home (familial condition), will look to the gang for empowerment (payoff). The gang offers this sense of power, through violence, and the fear it inflicts in others (specific behavior). As the sense of empowerment grows, the youth gang member develops a greater involvement with his gang (level of commitment). To disengage this youth, appropriate matching and alternatives are critical.

> "Volunteer programs and more job openings for teenagers." *(Moniqua, 16, Inner City)*

> "Build a place for teenagers to go and hang out during the weekends." *(Jake, 16, Rural)*

> "Have wholesome activities and 'safe areas' for kids to have fun." *(Karen, 17, Urban)*

> "Give them after-school activities to help keep them off the street." *(Thelma, 17, Urban)*

> "Have that person talk to a former gang member to learn how he got out." *(John, 16, Rural)*

Framework for Disengagement

Disengagement is a difficult step for a gang member. Its success depends on a team effort—the youth, the family, and others with special skills to help with the disengagement process. Dan Korem, in *Suburban Gangs: The Affluent Rebels* (1994), offers an eight-point strategy to help disengage youths from their gangs.

1. *Appoint a strategist.* Often, parents are not able to formulate a strategy because of their emotional involvement, lack of knowledge about the issue, and other barriers. A *strategist* can identify and answer the basic questions about the youth's gang involvement and come up with ideas to approach the troubled child. This person should have common sense and calmness under pressure, be able to understand the particular issues, have a balanced perspective, have the ability to relate to young people, and have the skill to design a short-term disengagement plan.

2. *Establish effective communication.* Foremost, the strategist must be able to build trust with the youth. This will help develop a style of communication between them, which will require the strategist to speak the language of the youth.

3. *Examine the facts.* The strategist first must determine if the youth is a gang member. Once this is known, the strategist must discern the reasons for membership, the alleged gang payoff, the nature of activities, and the level of involvement. It is crucial to gather all the facts related to gang membership as soon as possible. This will help the strategist in recommending action and diverting anxiety.

4. *Develop a preliminary strategy for resolving the problem.* This strategy needs to reduce the danger to the youth or other affected youths. It should also establish communication with the youth. In addition, it is essential that the plan identify reasons for the youth to disengage from the gang.

5. *Implement and fine-tune a long-term strategy.* This should achieve several long-term goals:

   —Permanent removal of the threat of harm to the youth and others.

   —Identification and resolution of the reasons the youth felt compelled him or her to join the gang.

   —Strengthening of healthy family relationships.

   —Positive alternatives to gang activity and involvement.

   —Effective discipline when necessary.

   —Guidance to help the youth plan a long-term future.

6. *Utilize a system of checks and balances.* Sometimes it is helpful for the

people involved to have input from unaffected people, or people who are not directly involved with the disengagement.

7. *Ask for professional help when needed.* Professionals such as mental health workers, law enforcement officers and school counselors are often the first ones to spot negative youth trends. Based on their experience, they can be helpful when the situation goes beyond what the strategist and others involved can handle alone.

8. *Employ necessary follow-up.* Families and other supporters need to provide ongoing monitoring. This is critical to help the youth maintain a gang-free life and grow a productive future.

CULTURAL SENSITIVITY

For any gang prevention or intervention program to succeed, it must incorporate *cultural sensitivity.* It also must be relevant to the ethnic and racial groups being targeted.

Indicators

Everything of importance starts with a definition. The definition for cultural sensitivity is complex and far-reaching. According to Arnold P. Goldstein and C. Ronald Huff, editors of *The Gang Intervention Handbook* (1993), cultural sensitivity refers to:

> A person's or a program's objective understanding, appraisal, appreciation, and knowledge of a particular cultural group. This awareness is used equitably in behavioral dispositions toward members of that group. Cultural sensitivity is developed through self-awareness, and elimination of stereotypes and unfounded views. It is acquired through objective knowledge about, and actual interaction with, members of a particular cultural group.

Communication

Gang-intervention efforts need clear and effective communication with the gang members, both verbal and nonverbal, or behavioral, communication.

Verbal communication is an obvious yet often overlooked barrier to the development of culturally sensitive intervention programs. It is important to note, however, that a staff member's ability to speak a particular language—or the gang member's ability to speak English—does not preclude communication problems. Effective communication involves much more than speaking the same language.

"Don't just talk to them. Listen!" *(Geneva, 14, Inner City)*

"Get out of buildings and into the community and talk to them." *(Moria, 16, Urban)*

Most communication—ninety-three percent—is nonverbal. Words comprise the remaining seven percent, therefore, it is critical to learn the nuances of nonverbal communication.

Staff Ethnicity

Just because a program employs a staff with the same cultural background, ethnicity, or race does not ensure that the staff is culturally sensitive to gang members and their issues. This stereotyping presumes that all people of a certain ethnic group or race have the same background, experiences, values, attitudes, beliefs, and expectations. This is not true.

Certainly, at a primary level, shared ethnicity or race might facilitate rapport-building. However, it will not necessarily sustain that rapport. In fact, it is important not to overlook other workers—non-ethnic minority individuals—who might be more culturally sensitive.

Essential Components

People who want to succeed in developing, administering, and maintaining prevention and intervention programs must make a total commitment to cultural sensitivity. This requires mastery of three essential components.

The youth gang worker needs a strong dose of *cultural awareness*—an assessment of attitudes, opinions, and assumptions regarding a particular culture. Also needed is *knowledge*—the facts about a culture's history, social position, values, norms, and beliefs, and *skill*—the stage at which a person becomes aware of oneself and knowledgeable about a particular cultural group. Skill allows the person to apply this knowledge effectively when interacting with members of that group.

Just because a person learns something specific about an ethnic or a racial group does not ensure that the person has developed a cultural sensitivity about them. Acquiring new information does not necessarily mean that the worker will accept—or respect—that information, or enter it into his or her personal belief system.

Therefore, merely providing information does not automatically translate into cultural sensitivity. However, if the new information does build on prior knowledge that is similar, then the likelihood of acceptance is greater. It is easier for workers to accept that which is familiar or compatible with what they already know.

How does this relate to gangs? Learning about the total impact of gangs on the youth's life will help the worker develop a better understanding of the gang member in terms of human needs and broader cultural influences.

> "Show trust. Don't be so scared to step out the door. Don't stare. Get involved. Get to know people in *their* neighborhoods." *(Selena, 15, Suburban)*

> "Provide help and assistance to troubled youths who are in gangs and want more than anything to get out." *(Zach, 17, Urban)*

Gang members are viewed as outsiders to society. They are considered unfit to participate in a civilized world. Yet youth gangs serve a specific role in members' socialization and provide a needed support system.

Sensitivity to ethnic and racial gang members requires adopting a more complex view of gang members than that which predominates law enforcement. Gang members have multiple social roles and multiple identities, many of which cross into the mainstream world, such as being legitimately employed. Youth gang workers need to understand and appreciate these varied identities and subcultures and not focus on gang membership only. Of course, knowledge of the member's individual role within the gang is crucial. Often, former gang members are used in gang prevention and intervention programs because they have this needed cultural sensitivity.

Certainly cultural sensitivity incorporates the lives and lifestyles of diverse people. It is always in flux and a mode of change, just as the people within the group change. This means that the workers who interact with gang members must retain a high degree of open-mindedness as the members and gang life itself evolve with time and circumstances.

> "They should have regular neighborhood conferences on gang prevention. Listen to what the kids in the hood have to say." *(Trey, 18, Inner City)*

Chapter Highlights

- Historically, four strategies addressed the youth gang problem in America:
  —Local community organization and mobilization.
  —Social intervention and youth outreach.
  —Social and economic opportunities provision.
  —Suppression.
- *Prevention* of gang involvement, like anything else that affects the entire community, requires a total community commitment.
- Key principles in intervention include:
  —Strengthening families.
  —Supporting core social institutions.
  —Promoting prevention strategies that reduce the impact of risk factors.
  —Creating a wide range of graduated sanctions.
  —Identifying and restraining serious, violent, and chronic juvenile offenders.
- For any prevention or intervention program to work, gang members must believe in them.
- Most gang members give three viable reasons for avoiding gang membership:
  —Being informed about the *risks* of membership.
  —Having families that impose and monitor *effective sanctions*.
  —Having access to *viable alternatives*, such as sports activities, jobs, and education.
- *One-on-one interventions*, which are tailored to each specific individual, provide the best chance for successfully disengaging youths from gangs.
- *Disengagement* often requires the involvement of the gang member's family and outsiders with the knowledge and ability to assist in the process.
- A disengagement strategy might involve the following steps:
  —Appoint a *strategist*.
  —Establish effective communication.
  —Examine the facts.
  —Develop a preliminary strategy for resolving the problem.
  —Implement and fine-tune a long-term strategy.

—Utilize a system of checks and balances.

—Ask for professional help when needed.

—Employ necessary follow-up and support.

- For any gang prevention or intervention program to succeed, it must incorporate *cultural sensitivity*. This component must be relevant to the ethnic and racial groups being targeted.

- Gang intervention efforts need clear and effective communication—verbal and nonverbal—between gang members and the intervenor.

- At a primary level, shared ethnicity or race might facilitate rapport-building, but it is no guarantee that cultural sensitivity exists for the intervenor.

- Components essential to cultural sensitivity are:

  —*Cultural awareness*—an assessment of attitudes, opinions, and assumptions regarding a particular culture.

  —*Knowledge*—the facts about a culture's history, social position, values, norms, and beliefs.

  —*Skill*—the stage at which a person becomes aware of oneself and knowledgeable about a particular cultural group.

- Just because a person learns something about an ethnic or a racial group does not guarantee that this person has developed a cultural sensitivity about its members.

- Sensitivity to racial and ethnic gang members requires adopting a more complex view of gang members and an awareness of the multiple identities—including mainstream—each gang member has.

- Workers who interact with gang members must retain a high degree of open-mindedness as the members and gang life itself evolve with time and circumstances.

Chapter 9

Law Enforcement

Though young as I am,
I know of the imperfections of our world.
No courtesy, not even a "Thank you, ma'am."
The laws don't serve us as they should.

My image is of innocence and naivete;
My insides are anything but . . .
Torn between two worlds, not knowing what I am to be.
Not wanting to see, I close my eyes, struggling to keep them
    shut.

Jennifer, 18, Urban

TACTICS AND APPROACHES

Effective gang *suppression*—punishing, often incarcerating, gang members for their illegal activities—is a necessary component in resolving the gang problem in this country. Yes, prevention and early intervention are preferred methods of involvement. However, when more seasoned gang members are involved, especially hard core gangsters, suppression is necessary. This most often involves law enforcement.

Police, Gangs, and Suppression

The relationship between law enforcement and gangs is ordinarily a strained one. It is not uncommon to blame—directly and indirectly—a worsening gang problem on various law enforcement activities, especially those involving suppression.

> "They should stop harassing kids for no apparent reason." *(Trey, 18, Inner City)*

> "Go after true killers and not the pot smokers." *(Brandon, 16, Inner City)*

> "Stop finding the bad in people and stop bringing kids down. We need more 'hands on' in the classroom and on the street. We need positive involvement with the police." *(Louise, 17, Urban)*

> "Don't arrest us for casual activities." *(Nicholas, 18, Rural)*

> "Arresting kids obviously makes things worse. We need more 'safe houses.' " *(Selena, 15, Suburban)*

The traditional police approach to gangs has been suppression, though, for a brief period, this was tempered with softer strategies of prevention and early intervention. Often these policies do not originate in the law enforcement organization itself. Rather, state legislatures and agencies create mandates that local law enforcement is obligated to follow. Suppression has been a popular mandate as the cry of "Do the crime, do the time" has evolved as a way to pacify entire communities that fear gang violence. In the youth survey for this book, respondents—at a nearly three-to-one ratio—wanted "very strong enforcement of current laws" and/or "tougher laws."

> "Law enforcement should strictly impose the law on youth gangs. They need to set the example to others that their behavior is not tolerated." *(Zach, 17, Urban)*

> "Enforcement of punishment for violent acts done by gang members." *(Olivia, 21, Urban)*

> "Get rid of the gangs! Reprimand gang members severely." *(Chanel, 16, Suburban)*

"Set harder punishment for gang members who commit crimes or are affiliated with gangs." *(Brian, 16, Urban)*

"Make it hard for people to get guns. For example, only let people over twenty-six years old, without children, buy them. If they do have kids, make them have a safe place in the home to hide the gun." *(Selena, 15, Suburban)*

"Make penalties for gang members who commit crimes harsher than those imposed on other people who commit crimes." *(Natasha, 16, Suburban)*

"Maintain a strict code of intolerance of youth gang behavior. Do not allow youth gang gatherings. The law shouldn't be so lax that youth gangs can 'get away with' illegal activities and senseless offenses due to their age." *(Zach, 17, Urban)*

"Lock them up." *(Janine, 17, Suburban)*

"Put them in detention centers." *(Jodi, 17, Urban)*

"Keep arresting them at all times. No freebies." *(Ray, 17, Urban)*

"Act tough on gang crime. This means harder sentences, bigger fines, community service for members caught in minor crimes. More 'scared straight' programs." *(Maria, 15, Urban)*

Police, as well as prosecutors and probation officers, sometimes use more creative suppression tactics. These might include, but are not limited to:

- Saturation-policing—concentrating police personnel in particular areas where gang activities are high, and the need for prominent and visible policing is necessary to curb these activities.
- Gang-oriented victim-witness protection programs—offering certain protections to youths who provide inside information about dangerous and illegal gang activities and the members who are involved.
- Seizure of assets—the taking by law enforcement of assets they suspect were the products or results of criminal activities.

Gang Control

Typical law enforcement organizations are not well structured to handle youth gangs. But this is changing as the growth of gangs permeates virtually every American community.

In the past several years, special forms of *gang control* have emerged in law enforcement. *Youth service programs* often involve police officers who are assigned to gang-control responsibilities, along with other duties. *Gang details* usually comprise one or more officers of a traditional unit who are assigned exclusive responsibility for gang control. *Gang units* have one or more officers assigned to a unit established solely to cope with gang problems.

Whatever its form, these efforts at gang control focus on four types of police activities: intelligence and information processing, prevention, enforcement, and follow-up investigation.

COMMUNITY POLICING

Increasingly, law enforcement is becoming aware of the need for community involvement and interagency collaborations in addressing gang problems. Communities, especially the police, have awakened to the reality that youth gangs cannot be eliminated—and the gang problem resolved—simply by jailing all gang members.

Working Together

The police recognize that they need to do more than they have done in the past to engage the community in the overall task of policing. *Community involvement* helps establish cooperative and meaningful relationships between the police and community members, which are essential to gang violence prevention.

One of the primary problems with relying totally on law enforcement for solutions is the dependency it creates within the community. When the community shares in the responsibility to resolve the issue, the entire community owns the problem—and the solution!

Community policing requires a total commitment from law enforcement officers to involve average citizens as partners in the process of reducing and controlling the contemporary problems of crime, drugs, fear of crime, and neighborhood decay. Its success depends on everyone working together to improve the overall quality of life in the community. To be totally responsive to—and responsible for—the idea of community policing, law enforcement must invite the involvement of other, non-police justice system agencies and organizations.

The goal of community policing is to promote the achievement of a stable and functional community. In a healthy community, life, work, religion, education, law enforcement, and other institutions reflect and reinforce common values. Recognizing these as positive goals, more than 11,000 communities in the United States have community-oriented policing services.

Community policing might include school-based lecture programs, school and probation liaisons, recreation, and job programs. It can also involve the family of the gang members with counseling, social service referral opportunities, family development programs, and more.

> "Have support groups for young people who need help from adults." *(Dana, 16, Rural)*

> "Community organizations need to show youths they care by providing places where the kids can go to talk and have support." *(Elia, 17, Inner City)*

> "Run a gang-free club." *(Nikki, 17, Suburban)*

> "Offer alternative programs or groups that specialize in positive activities." *(Marianne, 17, Urban)*

> "Start a gangs anonymous program so kids can understand life and find support from others who are going through the same thing." *(Richard, 19, Urban)*

Evolving Police Role

As community policing evolves, so will the law enforcement officers who participate in it. Their newer role involves tactics of suppression and social intervention. Their job still necessitates proper prosecution and conviction of violent and dangerous youths. However, they also strive to prevent youth gang crime, help members leave the gang, and work toward a healthier, safer community.

Today's police officer might help a youth get a job, counsel another in school, or refer still another to specific social services . . . none of this will succeed if law enforcement officers do not learn how to communicate with youth gang members in ways that demonstrate respect, acceptance, and concern for and appreciation of the gang youth.

> "Listen to gangbangers. Let them tell you why they broke laws and hurt people." *(Jamie, 15, Inner City)*

> "Talk to teens. Show them that you care and are there to help them." *(Marisela, 16, Rural)*

> "Get to know them. Help them, one by one." *(Jackie, 16, Urban)*

> "Be available to listen to troubled youths, on and off campus. Provide protection for those who are constant victims of gang violence." *(Zach, 17, Urban)*

> "Quit being so hard on gangs. Instead of trying to prevent them, accept them." *(Jerry, 15, Inner City)*

> "Don't treat kids like gang members until you're sure they are." *(Ed, 16, Inner City)*

> "Protect kids who are trying to leave gangs." *(Sarah, 16, Suburban)*

When community policing places officers within neighborhoods, it encourages these officers to work with community residents to solve their problems on a daily basis. Children and families have regular contact with officers in a wide variety of helping roles, far beyond the context of traditional law enforcement, which allows relationships of trust to grow between the police and the families and youths within the neighborhoods.

> "Educate parents and youths about what a gang is and the negative effects it can have on a child." *(Christopher, 18, Urban)*

> "Go into the schools and talk to kids about gangs." *(Adam, 14, Inner City)*

"Have youth groups sponsored by the gang unit." *(Moniqua, 16, Inner City)*

"Help kids of all races, not just the rich ones." *(Lacharles, 17, Inner City)*

"Give programs on violence awareness." *(Lynn, 20, Rural)*

"Stop things before they happen. Do everything you can to prevent a full-blown gang from even starting." *(Tonya, 17, Rural)*

Community policing gives police officers the opportunity to maximize positive experiences with youths. Police officers who take on a consistent, authoritative presence in their neighborhoods can serve as positive role models—even heroes—for young people for whom there are too few positive adult role models in their lives.

These programs work. According to a 1998 National Institute of Justice and Carnegie Corporation national study, community-oriented policing services—in collaboration with youth-serving organizations—provide substantial help in keeping kids out of trouble.

THE COURTS AND BEYOND

Juvenile courts often have difficulty dealing with gang problems. With regularity, resources needed to help judges develop the legal expertise to handle these issues are not available.

Judicial Jurisdiction

Nationally, there is a movement toward more punitive and suppressive judicial actions in gang-related crimes. In some juvenile court jurisdictions, however, judges are utilizing their courts as centers for coordinated rehabilitative approaches. These involve a collaborative effort of the community and its schools, families, for-profit and nonprofit organizations, law enforcement, and the courts.

Just as with other adolescent issues, children are often more alike than different. The courts have been slow to understand the likenesses. It is important, therefore, for the courts to appreciate—and act on—the fact that the violent and aggressive behaviors of gang youths are often responses to the same issues that other deprived, problematic, and troublesome youths might have. This does not mean judges should overlook the severity of the issues . . . just to understand that the sources of these behaviors are more similar than they might want to believe, accept, or address.

Often, because of the nature of their crimes and the overload of the juvenile justice system, judges *certify* gang members as adults. The certification can have a substantial impact. Juvenile court judges have two options with kids: detain them or release them to their parents or guardians. Adult court judges can detain, set bail, and release a suspect or defendant. One alternative to the existing system would be the development of pre-trial services. These would provide both social services and controls for selected, chronically violent gang youths awaiting trial.

Judicial proceedings are particularly difficult when they involve gang members. Often other gang members come to court and distract the proceedings with hand signals, symbols, and other gang-related behaviors. The accuracy of testimonies by witnesses who are members of an opposing gang also needs close scrutiny. Gang members might manipulate testimony to falsely incriminate a suspect, or they might withhold evidence that could result in the dismissal of charges.

Sentencing is probably the most critical function a juvenile court judge performs. Not only does the length of sentence impact the defendant, it affects that person's family and the victims and their families. Many judges are looking for *alternative sentencing* options. These might include a menu of choices: house arrest, intensive supervision, fines and community service, or restorative justice. Whatever the choices, a continuum of punishment and treatment can be formulated and implemented to contribute to *rehabilitation* for many youths who might otherwise face only the option of incarceration. Ultimately, the judge must weigh the sentence according to the youth's ability to rehabilitate, the crime, and the need to protect the community.

> "Give more off-site counseling instead of always locking kids up." *(Cole, 16, Inner City)*

> "Create programs for youth offenders to do community service and other things, rather than sending non-gang members to gang-filled jails." *(Olivia, 21, Urban)*

Most gang youths do not remain members after their teen years, though this is changing with socioeconomic, familial, and other pressures. Therefore, juvenile judges can play a major role in gang intervention. They need to ask essential questions to learn how to deal with the youths before their courts.

- Is this youth ready to get out of the gang?
- What can we do to transition this youth out of the gang?
- What community support will it take to accomplish this transition?
- How quickly can we accomplish this?
- What kinds of alternatives can we offer to ensure that the youth stays out of the gang?
- What forms of community-based care should we provide for the youth and his or her family?

Judges also have the option to put the youth on *probation*. This decision to release the child, usually under specific conditions, would be based on ensuring the protection of the community, the restitution for the victim, and the delivery of suitable services to the youth and his or her immediate family. To enhance the likelihood of success, judges often issue *special orders*. These might require the adolescent to avoid gang-related behaviors and activities, to stay away from gang members themselves, to observe curfews, to perform community service, and so on. Family counseling often is required as well.

> "Show them what it's like by picking them up and having them spend the night in jail." *(Heather, 15, Rural)*

> "Talk to them about all the people they see killed and how they got killed." *(Eric, 16, Suburban)*

When a judge does send a gang member to prison, the hope is that the youth will disengage from gang activities. However, if the correctional facility does not offer alternatives—education, vocational training, social skills development—the likelihood of the youth returning to the gang after imprisonment is substantial. Unfortunately, too many juvenile institutions are actually used as gang-recruiting environments. If the teenagers were not gang members when they arrived at the facility, many will become so before they leave.

Community-Based Care

Of course, the hope is for the youth to return home to start a new life. *Community-based care* is crucial to a successful transition back to mainstream community life. Support systems and continuity, education, job training, substance abuse counseling, peer relationship development, activity alternatives, and personal dispute resolution classes are just some of the community-based care components for the juvenile's movement to a more productive life.

> "Make some kind of effort for those who have been, or are, incarcerated to be able to study a career or do more things for the community." *(Nereyda, 17, Urban)*

For those returning to their own gang-infested neighborhoods, electronic monitoring often helps them separate from their gangs. Electronic monitoring can deter peer pressure because gangs do not want their activities—or those of their members—monitored.

For younger offenders, day treatment programs offer hope. With a place to go, and people who care, these young people learn to replace the sense of family that the gang offered. Of course, long-term success requires that the youth's own family, especially his or her parents, become involved in the programs as well.

Chapter Highlights

- It is not uncommon to blame—directly and indirectly—a worsening gang problem on various law enforcement activities, especially those involving suppression.
- Typical law enforcement organizations are not well structured to handle youth gangs.
- In the past several years, special forms of *gang control* have emerged in law enforcement, including, but not limited to, *youth service programs, gang details,* and *gang units.*
- Gang-control efforts focus on four types of police activities: intelligence and information processing, prevention, enforcement, and follow-up investigations.
- *Community involvement* helps establish cooperative and meaningful rela-

tionships between the police and community members, which is essential to gang violence prevention.

- *Community policing* requires a total commitment from law enforcement officers to involve average citizens as partners in the process of reducing and controlling the contemporary problems of crime, drugs, fear of crime, and neighborhood decay.

- As community policing evolves, so will the law enforcement officers who participate in it. Their success will depend heavily on how well they communicate and interact with youth gang members.

- Juvenile courts often have difficulty dealing with gang problems, often because necessary resources are limited.

- Because of the nature of their crimes and the overload of the juvenile justice system, judges often *certify* gang members as adults.

- *Sentencing*, the most critical function of the juvenile court judge, significantly affects all parties involved in the legal action.

- A continuum of punishment and treatment could contribute to *rehabilitation* for many youths who might otherwise face only the option of incarceration.

- Judges also have the option of putting youths on *probation*.

- *Special orders* can require the adolescent to avoid gang-related behaviors and activities, stay away from gang members, observe curfews, perform community service, and so on.

- *Community-based care* is crucial to a successful transition back to mainstream community life.

Chapter 10

Schools

Harmonizing relationships.
> Making a person feel better.

Explaining how to do something,
> A person learns something to be used later in life.

Lifting spirits.
> Making a person feel that he or she is not alone.

Problems solved more easily.
> Leaving less strain on the person.

Flooding the helpless with hope.
> Encouraging others to help.

Used anywhere, anytime.
> A gift everyone wants to have.

Leaves less bad feeling toward others.
> Letting them know that there are people who will help them.

Mark, 14, Suburban

SCHOOL ENVIRONMENT

In addition to neighborhood influences and motivations, a wide range of school-related experiences contributes to a youth's positive outlook toward gangs. Many gang members attend schools; gang activity is a community concern that has overflowed to school campuses. However, once at school sites, gangs and gang activity are educator and support-staff problems.

Elementary School Impact

Even in the earliest grades, it is easier for some children to have ongoing contact and interaction with schoolmates who already belong to or hang out with gangs. Because of these affiliations, teachers and others often label these youngsters as deviants and troublemakers. In turn, many of these children seek out others similarly labeled for comfort and acceptance. Such labels often prompt the children to perpetuate the stereotype connected to the labels. Thus the children act out the negative behaviors that others expect them to have.

> "Stop assuming and blaming young children who aren't in gangs for being in gangs. This is exactly what will lead them to gang affiliation." *(Jerry, 17, Suburban)*

Being rejected early in life by mainstream society—and labeled negatively—produces a profound and long-lasting effect. Rejection can be incapacitating by denying the child his or her individuality and integrity.

> "Talk with kids at school and help gang members. Don't make them outcasts." *(Raymond, 17, Urban)*

> "Don't look at people and put them in little sections or groups." *(Kristina, 17, Urban)*

For many of these outcasts, entering into associations with other labeled and/or mistreated peers represents their first official connection with gang behavior. What impact does this have on their connection with school? During their childhood and teen years, the institution of education and the people it involves—teachers, counselors, administrators—often serve as antagonists rather than facilitators in their development.

Safe Schools: Responding to Violence

For children to progress and develop in positive ways, schools need to be safe. In late 1998, I was selected as the only state legislator in the country to attend the first "White House Conference on School Safety." At that conference, U.S. Secretary of Education Richard Riley released a report that stated that ninety percent of our nation's schools are free of serious crimes. However, the number of gangs has nearly doubled since 1990.

When violence replaces safety, both educators and students are at risk of injury and sometimes death. Certainly a society that values its citizens cannot tolerate a climate in which they are placed at such risk. It is important to remember that schools are not isolated environments. They reflect what is happening in the rest of the world, starting with the communities in which they sit. It also is essential to monitor all levels of violence in these various environments.

Many children today identify themselves and their relationships only through conflict. A substantial percentage of our children have been traumatized—experienced violence at some level. Once this happens, they are denied a certain level of coping skills. So what might seem insignificant or "child's play"—pushing and shoving, hurtful name calling, harassment—can easily lead to more severe behavior when left unchecked. Violence is violence.

> "Bring gang unit officers to school to talk to them and show the students pictures of what violence really does to people. Have them bring in guys doing time to explain what it's like to be locked up." *(Cassandra, 15, Inner City)*

> "Get former gang members to talk to kids about how horrible gangs are. Kids need to see the actuality of it all." *(Chanel, 16, Suburban)*

> "Ex-gang members can scare kids into not wanting to live their lives in violent ways." *(Janine, 17, Suburban)*

Certainly violence impairs the teaching and learning process. Schools are not war zones. Their function is to create places where teaching, learning, and other socialization can occur safely and productively. Ironically, schools are often the safest places for children to spend their time.

The physical environment must be safe. To ensure this, many schools start with the idea that the school is a safe and neutral zone. This means that neither gang confrontations nor intimidation of other students will be allowed to occur on or near campus.

> "Sometimes you have to get tougher, and tougher. For starters, add more school police." *(Q.B., 15, Inner City)*

Schools might also have metal detectors, eliminate lockers, provide better lighting, improve the appearance of the school (graffiti removal), and offer on-site policing. They might prohibit students access to their cars, beepers, and cellular telephones during school hours. Many schools limit and supervise the entry, movement, and exit of persons on the school grounds and within school buildings.

More and more, schools are requiring students to wear uniforms, which promote a less materialistic learning environment and allow schools to monitor the presence of undesirable people on campus.

> "With a form of uniform, you'll be able to establish a visual acknowledgment of a youth gang and . . . be able to prevent them." *(Marianne, 17, Urban)*

> "No gang member should be allowed to wear the same uniforms as other kids in the school." *(Wayne, 15, Urban)*

> "A dress code should be enforced. Don't allow clubs to form." *(Raylene, 17, Inner City)*

Working with law enforcement officers to track crimes in the school is also important. Many officers are teaching parents about the early warning signs of gang involvement and the need for sharing time with their children. Others are enforcing the national policy of "zero tolerance" for juveniles who carry or use weapons on campus; and still others are adding an assessment component to discover the reasons and possible resolutions for carrying weapons.

> "Make sure they know the dangers. Educate them and let them know there is no gang tolerance in school." *(Jackie, 16, Urban)*

> "Zero tolerance for gang activity!" *(Richard, 19, Urban)*

CREATIVE SOLUTIONS

For the long term, schools are adopting multiple uses for their campuses. They are increasing the use of their buildings as community resource centers for community activities to enhance community ownership. Community and business partnerships also provide valuable long-term alternatives to gang involvement. It is especially important to provide safe alternatives in the after-school hours between 2:00 P.M. and midnight when idle or unsupervised children are most likely to get into trouble. A coordinated commitment to change needs total community involvement.

Assimilation

One such creative alternative requires acceptance. Communities need to accept the reality that totally dissolving gangs is highly unlikely. Therefore, the approach that can work with these intact groups involves *assimilation*.

Traditional student organizations provide their members with opportunities to share information, time, space, activities, and more. Most of these activities involve the school and its staff. They are encouraged and are considered positive.

Youth gangs share most features of these school clubs, but gangs are viewed as negative. School officials do not affirm them, they do not have adult sponsors, and adults on campus do not encourage children to join them. These gangs are not encouraged to participate in schoolwide activities designed to foster school spirit, pride, and ownership.

> "Schools should push sporting events and positive activities. They should make it known and easy for a student to join a club or sports." *(Danna, 17, Urban)*

> "Get afternoon activities for kids to do. They need a place to hang out for a couple of hours." *(S.D., 16, Inner City)*

> "Take a poll and find out what most kids like to do and make a club for that particular thing." *(Jake, 16, Rural)*

> "Offer a diverse choice of sports teams, clubs, and activities that kids can be involved in and proud of." *(Maggie, 16, Urban)*

One novel approach—within the scope of real-world circumstances—requires school officials to find ways to foster the *mirroring* of school-sponsored and encouraged groups by those who belong to gangs. This is not an easy project. Yet this assimilation—even in small and incremental steps—can produce positive results. For example, the school can establish certain entrance criteria common for all school-based activities, such as minimum grades. As the mainstreaming evolves, adult sponsors must have a positive relationship with each youth gang member, recognize each youth's efforts, and focus on positive attributes.

Ongoing communication and interaction between all groups is essential. In addition, communication between the authority figures and youth gang members must occur in a non-threatening way. The desired results are positive relationship building and a safe school environment. Other forms of interaction can also help. These might involving the following:

- Scheduling conferences with youth gang members to let them know that the school is interested in them and their problems, and that the gang members have a channel of communication to school authorities.
- Assigning administrators and counselors to work directly with gang members and serve as mentors for them.
- Utilizing gang members in accepted on-campus roles of authority and responsibility, such as hall monitors, teachers' assistants, and campus guides.
- Providing opportunities for legitimate interaction between gang members and youths from other school-based groups to encourage healthy, non-threatening relationship building between the groups.

Personal Development Programs

Alternatives to gang involvement must be more than activity based. Often youths join gangs out of the frustrations they feel elsewhere in their lives.

Because most of these young people come from dysfunctional families, their own abilities to deal with conflict, pressure, anger, and violence are limited. Low self-esteem prevents them from knowing how to resolve their own problems.

Gangs generally teach dysfunctional youths how to handle their issues with violence. This involves the use of weapons most of the time. How can schools change this trend? They can do what the gangs have done—give vulnerable young people alternatives to resolve their frustrations and personal issues.

Anger management and *conflict resolution* programs help young people learn how to deal with their feelings and frustrations. These programs give young people tools to manage their lives, their personal conflicts, and their emotional upheavals. The *personal empowerment* that youths develop ultimately helps them learn how to apply these skills in diverse situations.

Peer mediation programs teach youths how to work with their contemporaries to resolve issues among themselves, which help them understand how to work together to solve problems in rational ways. These programs also incorporate consequences for behavior—reasonable consequences.

Peer resistance programs give youths the tools to say "no" to gang involvement. They help young people resist the negative influences of peers that lead to unacceptable and illegal behaviors. Peer resistance skills also help youths learn positive alternatives to fill the voids in their lives that gangs might otherwise satisfy—security, companionship, recognition, attachment, status, accomplishment.

> "Show them the statistics of gang members who graduate from high school. Only two people from my gang graduated." *(Pete, 16, Inner City)*

> "Provide open assistance and protection for members involved in gangs who are ready and willing to come out." *(Zach, 17, Urban)*

> "Educate kids about gangs and provide mentors for the kids who need help finding a positive direction." *(Tonya, 17, Rural)*

After-School Programs

Working families increasingly find it difficult to care for their children during the afternoon and early evening hours. In 1998, about thirty million children had parents who worked outside the home, yet many of these children did not have access to affordable, quality care during the hours before and after school.

Children and teens who are left unsupervised during these hours—often from 2:00 P.M. until midnight—are more likely to get involved with alcohol, drugs, and tobacco. They are also more likely than those involved in constructive activities to engage in criminal and other high-risk behaviors, to receive poor grades, and to drop out of school.

> "Night-time recreational activities in at-risk neighborhoods." *(Frank, 17, Suburban)*

> "Programs to support 'lost' kids." *(Russ, 18, Inner City)*

> "Keep kids in school longer each day." *(Kent, 15, Urban)*

Unfortunately, there is a chronic shortage of after-school programs to serve these children. Less than half of the children who need and want these programs have access to them. More than one-third of our nation's twelve-year-olds are left by themselves regularly while their parents are at work.

The value of after-school programs cannot be underestimated. For starters, they can provide positive environments and age-appropriate activities. They help children build academically on what they learn during regular school hours. Such programs help nurture healthy relationships between children and caring adults, all of this in a safe environment.

MAKING A COMMITMENT

One reason for the increase in violence in and around our schools involves supply and demand. Schools, with their ready supply of potential gang members, have become a prime recruiting ground.

School-Based Interventions

Schools are one place where recognition, prevention, and early intervention can help reduce gang activities, especially those involving violence. Outside the home, the school offers the greatest opportunity for positive, prolonged contact with all kinds of youth, including gang members.

Any kind of program or policy must begin with one reality: Denial of gangs does not solve the problems they create! Youth gangs and their oppressive activities increase when ignored. Even if no overt gang activity seems to be present in a school, administrators, teachers, and support staff need to check for signs of gang activity. Awareness of indicators is the first step toward gang control.

By understanding what membership provides for gang members, educators may be able to substitute equally rewarding and socially accepted activities. In the classroom, keys to success in reaching children involve rewards for particular group behavior. This approach avoids singling out individuals. Therefore, success occurs in group participation and cooperative classroom procedures, which include heavy doses of praise, reward, and good humor.

A successful preventive approach also builds self-esteem in each affected youth. It considers and addresses the reasons youths are drawn into gangs: fear, peer pressure, lack of education, poor employment skills, dysfunctional families, history of family gang involvement, and lack of alternatives. Preventive programs help reinforce socially constructive behavior and offer alternatives for employment, self-accountability, and lifestyle.

"Promote unity and provide counselors for troubled youths. Teach the dangers of gangs and help everyone feel as if they belong." *(Sarah, 16, Suburban)*

"Have good role models, counselors, and teachers." *(Felix, 16, Suburban)*

"Provide positive counseling and understanding about the issues. Address these with sensitivity and commitment." *(Christina, 17, Urban)*

"Be there for youths. Love them. Talk with them. Trust them with truth." *(Selena, 15, Suburban)*

"Convince them to go to school and get an education so they don't think they have to sell drugs to make money." *(Bill, 16, Inner City)*

"Offer a lot of clubs and peer help and counseling to kids who may lean towards joining gangs." *(Chanel, 16, Suburban)*

To ensure that school-based preventions and interventions can work, educators, administrators, and support staff must get everyone involved at some level. For example:

- Help students develop high self-esteem, often beginning with a sense of personal achievement. This encourages them to separate themselves from the group mind-set and to respect their own abilities to grow and sustain their own independent thinking and activity.
- Encourage students to work cooperatively with others, as individuals and groups, to solve problems.
- Offer students opportunities to make choices. Let them take the initiative and practice independence. Provide them with a variety of learning options.
- Avoid setting students up for criticism by their peers.
- Teach students how to accomplish specific tasks and set new goals upon their completion.
- Educate young people about the need to respect cultural diversity.

- Develop student contracts that encourage and reinforce positive behavior standards.
- Identify and pay close attention to known gang leaders. Maintain open and regular lines of communication—two-way communication—with them.

Activities involving others include, but are not limited to, the following:

- Offer gang seminars for parents. Educate them about ways to combat gang activity.
- Train all teachers and support staff. Teach them about gang signs and other indicators. Encourage them to report gang activity early.
- Increase security with law enforcement patrols or additional school security.
- Create collaborations with community organizations to provide positive alternatives—recreation, employment, education—to youths.

Of course, all efforts at prevention and intervention will not be successful. Regardless of the level of success, it is important for schools to involve parents. Parents can reinforce school discipline and increase the school staff's understanding of personal situations and conditions affecting the student. Of course, be aware that youths often hide their gang involvement from their parents or guardians.

Sometimes a youth's continuous misbehavior might require on-site suspension. Educators know that on-site suspensions can help provide supervision for students while resolving their problems. Education professionals know that sending children home—where they are often unsupervised—can actually contribute to the child's misbehavior or illegal activities.

Another option involves enrolling the troubled or disruptive child in an adjustment or alternative school, a community service project, or some other program. These programs are designed to remove a disruptive student from regular classes, to resolve the student's problems, and, hopefully, to return the student to regular classes.

Ultimately, when no other diversion programs work, it might be necessary to remove identified habitual offenders from regular school settings—the option is placement in a highly supervised, structured setting maintained by juvenile justice agencies.

"Kick them out." *(Janine, 17, Suburban)*

"Don't kick them out at all. This is more of a reward than a punishment." *(Ray, 17, Urban)*

"Expel anyone who is involved in any gang activities." *(Josh, 14, Rural)*

"Sometimes there is nothing you can do. My school, for example, was run by gangs." *(Nate, 19, Inner City)*

Ultimate Objectives

It would be foolish to think that schools have all the answers to school violence and gang life. However, each school can serve as a surrogate extended family to embrace all students, as long as these students respect this "family," its rights, and its property.

Schools can serve as a refuge for young people. In fact, schools might be the last refuge—a place where children can hold their own and find support against the overwhelming challenges outside the school gates. Therefore, schools should strive to respond to these cries from their students.

At the individual level, this means that school officials must create *gang awareness programs*. The school has a responsibility to heighten student awareness of the consequences of gang membership and involvement, in detail.

School officials must listen to each child. They must learn to understand the dysfunctional issues in that child's life. They must respond or intervene as quickly and as thoroughly as possible.

"Have gang awareness meetings and provide statistics of gang members in jails." *(Natasha, 16, Suburban)*

"Look out for students who are involved in gangs and observe them trying to recruit. Get involved before they take over." *(Maria, 15, Urban)*

"Teach kids the consequences of joining a gang." *(Moria, 16, Inner City)*

"Provide the statistics and information of local gang activity in the school district or even that particular school. Only by letting

others see the numbers will kids really understand the problem."
(Zach, 17, Urban)

"Have assemblies in which teenagers who have gangbanged and
been locked up come to speak to the kids." *(Tina, 17, Suburban)*

"It isn't the school's responsibility to remove kids from gangs.
Their only job is to educate and provide enriching activities that
might interest kids." *(Olivia, 21, Urban)*

"Let all the children know when their classmate dies in gang-
related activities." *(Pete, 16, Inner City)*

According to Sharon F. Kissane, in *Gang Awareness: What You Can Do*
(1995), changes made in the schools, especially in the inner-city schools,
should accomplish three objectives:

1. Ensure a safe environment for students.
2. Provide an adequate education to students.
3. Retain students long enough to provide them with an adequate education. Schools must help them compete in a job market that increasingly
   requires educational credentials, fundamental literacy, and mathematics
   skills.

In a 1998 presentation, "Reconnecting with Our Children and Keeping
Them Safe," Secretary Riley focused on the need for personal commitment
to our nation's children. He referred to a 1997 survey by the American
Medical Association (AMA) in which 90,000 young people shared their own
concerns. The AMA survey indicated that young people who felt connected
to their parents and schools were less likely to engage in high-risk behavior.
Basically, kids who feel connected to school are more likely to feel connected
at home. Children who perform better in school generally learn about the
value of school at home. What does this mean? According to Riley:

• Every school in the nation must actively engage and encourage parents to
  do whatever they can to buffer the time demands of daily living so that
  parents stay connected to their children. Educators must help parents learn
  and appreciate that the rewards of staying connected far outweigh the
  rewards of "busyness."

- Educators must make a commitment to the children at an individual level. Simply, this means that each child in school in America must have a positive and caring relationship with at least one adult.

- Each school—and the entire community that it involves and affects—must make a commitment to go the distance to ensure that every child and every family feels connected and valued.

Chapter Highlights

- In addition to neighborhood influences and motivations, a wide range of school-related experiences contributes to a youth's positive outlook toward gangs.

- Being rejected early by mainstream society—and labeled negatively—produces a profound, long-lasting effect on children.

- For children to progress and develop in positive ways, schools need to be safe.

- Schools are supposed to function as places where teaching, learning, and other socialization can occur safely and productively.

- Gangs share most features of traditional and accepted school organizations; however, gangs are viewed as negative.

- Open, two-way communication between authority figures and gang members must occur in a nonthreatening way to produce a safe school environment.

- Alternatives to gang involvement must be more than activity based. Examples of essential esteem-building programs include *anger management, conflict resolution, peer mediation*, and *peer resistance.*

- Children and teens who are left unsupervised during the afternoon and early evening hours are more likely to get involved with alcohol, drugs, and tobacco. They are also more inclined toward criminal behavior, poor grades, and dropping out of school.

- Schools are one place where recognition, prevention, and early intervention can help reduce gang activities.

- Any kind of program or policy must begin with one reality: Denial of youth gangs does not solve the problems that they create!

- A successful preventive approach builds self-esteem in each affected youth, which requires understanding the reasons youths are drawn to gangs: fear, peer pressure, lack of education, poor employment skills, dysfunctional families, history of gang involvement in the family, and a lack of alterna-tives.

- Programs of prevention and intervention help reinforce socially construc-tive behavior by offering alternatives for employment, self-accountability, and lifestyle.

- When prevention and intervention do not succeed, youths might be sus-pended, enrolled in adjustment schools, or incarcerated.

- Schools do not have all the answers to school violence and gang life. However, they can provide a sense of surrogate family to embrace all students, as long as these students respect this "family," its rights, and its property.

- Research proves that children who feel connected to school are more likely to feel connected at home. Children who perform better in school gen-erally learn about the value of school at home.

Chapter 11

The Media

A sea of masks surround us
    As if ebbing in at the tide.
Then night slithers slowly in,
    And the masks turn to hide.

The masks ornately painted,
    Each one seeming more vain.
Yet, the masks are emotionless,
    All the expressions are the same.

All are equipped with mouths.
    Yet, they lack a set of ears.
No use for communication.
    For none of them ever hears.

Thus, the lifeless brooding masks
    Remain alone and confined,
Thinking they know each other's mask,
    When truly they are blind.

Kimberly, 18, Urban

THE MEDIA DOMAIN

Increasingly we experience the impact of the media in shaping the thoughts
and actions of our children and teenagers. Television, radio, movies, videos,

interactive computers, and other sources of entertainment are exerting influence over their abilities to think and act for themselves.

Television programs since the 1990s have particularly reflected societal changes, such as shared parenting, single parenting, minority issues, social conflicts, and emotional challenges. The historic *Murphy Brown* set a television precedent in which a single-mother news anchor shared the parenting of her infant son with a male artist. Other programs, such as the late 1990s television hit *ER*, reflect contemporary viewers' demands for reality. High-tech camera work, creative and fast-paced editing, and reality-based story lines positioned that series' ratings at the top.

For the sake of argument, let us consider two options about the impact of the media. One possibility points to television as something that mirrors us more than it molds us. If so, we are beginning to revolt against the television's idealized images of domestic life. Yet, at the same time, it often strives to embrace flawed families with happy and hopeful endings, even if the story lines are tough.

Children's literature reflects change as well. Authors and artists are designing books that mirror the emerging family sentiment of consensual love and the value of autonomy. However, unless this message is handled responsibly, children might absorb lethal doses of disturbing material.

Of course, the definition of media has expanded in directions unforeseen, even in the 1970s and early 1980s. Video games, interactive computers, and virtual-reality experiences have emerged as the media of choice for many young people, and older ones as well.

Unfortunately, many of the themes of these games are based on aggression and violence. Like television, video games perpetuate—rather than nix—stereotypes about people, especially women, minorities, and the less able.

DEFINED BY TELEVISION

Television—not just its advertising and programs—has taken on a greater-than-life presence in our lives, having influenced our children in virtually every way. Television has taught them the advantages of microwave "zapping" versus a real home-cooked meal, made-for-TV movies versus reading literature, spending money on each other, versus spending time with each other.

> "Television shows, news, and commercials have given us unrealistic expectations about how we should live and what we should expect." *(Janelle, 14, Urban)*

The Saturation of Television

In my book *The Nesting Syndrome: Grown Children Living at Home* (1997), I discuss how television and other media have changed the way we look at our lives, our families, our careers, our relationships, and our other life choices. All media, especially television, have helped us glorify whatever is "new"; we think twice about getting involved with whatever is "seasoned." Television has provided young people with newfound relationships, however fictionalized, as substitutes for getting to know one another in the flesh.

It is not surprising to learn that the Roper Organization conducted studies in the early 1990s which revealed that the single activity Americans most look forward to each day is not human contact, but watching television. Even during dinner, at least half of the people prefer to watch television than to converse with their families.

In times of trouble, Americans of all ages rely on television to solve their woes. According to Ferenc Maté in *A Reasonable Life* (1993), thirty-five percent of American men who consider themselves depressed turn to television, rather than friends or family, to resolve their emotional issues. Some Americans consider television watching a social event, an interactive opportunity. They say television programs give us something to talk about, something to share with others. What did we do before we had strangers performing before us on a screen? Surely we were conversant with our families before the invention of television!

Human Attachment

Taken to the next level of involvement with the tube, some viewers develop attachments to fictional characters that surpass the ones they have with their own loved ones. At a time when divorce is higher than ever and dual-career families are cramping family time, high-tech alternatives compete for our time and energy. It is no wonder that our youths are finding comfort with the distance, yet safety, that *television* provides. It is pacifier in tough times; a friend in good ones; no judgment; no expectations; unfortunately, no human connection either.

Since television limits human interaction, our young people often make a choice. The more they invite this medium into their lives, the more they depend on it for their own thoughts and actions. They can grow to distrust their own ideas and instincts. They can too willingly accept what they are told, no questions asked. Without asking questions and challenging ideas, however, they slip backwards. They relinquish themselves.

This affects how our children learn as well. With the speedier delivery of visual images, our attention spans drop. In 1968, for example, the average sound bite or block of uninterrupted political speech ran forty-two seconds. In the late 1980s, the average attention span dropped to fewer than ten seconds. Today, videos on MTV regularly use edits as short as one-third of a second or less. The increase in images per second corresponds directly to an increase in the amount of visual information that younger viewers are capable of gleaning from the monitor.

Television continues to offer a variety of gratifications. It invites viewers to relax, to disregard their real-life problems, to surrender themselves to attractive screen people, and to become absorbed in events. This holds an extraordinary appeal for young people.

Addiction?

Many experts consider the television habit similar to an addiction, something viewers just cannot give up. This creates a total dependence on a medium that gives them daily direction in their lives. People spend as much as forty percent of their free time in front of a television set.

In *The Five Myths of Television Power* (1993), Douglas Davis considers the possibility of *television addiction*. Of nine criteria that occur in the diagnosis of substance abuse, television addiction might fit in several ways. Davis describes television addiction as "a substance often taken in larger amounts . . . than the person intended . . . and, with it, the viewer gives up important social occupations."

However, Davis believes that the idea of television addiction is really a myth, because audiences can choose between dependence and independence on the medium. By exercising the option to turn off the television, viewers can buck the alleged addiction. Unlike other addictions, viewers can make choices about when to participate and when not to. For children, especially those in dysfunctional families, however, television often serves as the only nurturer and friend in the home, the only thing they can depend on.

Even for those young people who watch television fifty or more hours a week, however, television can have the opposite of its intended effect. These young viewers can become numb to the medium and its messages. Remember the attention-span issue? Without visual stimulation and restimulation, boredom will set in. Therefore, rather than dwelling with full attention in front of the television set, as time passes most young people end up doing other things or leaving. Or, they often talk among themselves and ignore the television set completely.

> "I always have the television on when I do other things. It makes good background noise when I study, talk on the phone, and pop in and out of the house. It keeps me company." *(Doc Louis, 15, Suburban)*

THE MEDIA'S RESPONSIBILITY TO YOUNG AUDIENCES

As one of the most powerful, easily accessible, and ever-present influences in a youth's life, the media—especially television—have an extraordinary responsibility to use good judgment in their news, programming, and advertising. What will this take?

Programming

One simple but critical principle will continue to influence media decisions: profit. Even if we could eliminate the profit motive, this would not result in public ownership or control of what the media does or does not do.

Let us start with *entertainment.* The transmission of the message is not magical or mysterious. The power of the entertainment industry to influence actions of others emanates from its ability to redefine what constitutes normal behavior in this country. Young people take these entertainment role models seriously. Often, pop culture personalities, with enough clout and media exposure, can single-handedly initiate national trends, behaviors, and attitudes.

The American media appeal to their audiences through middle- and upper-class values by emphasizing personalities, personal celebrity, and individual achievement. They emphasize that status and personal qualities are vital in achieving success, and these messages are conveyed constantly in news, political coverage, entertainment, and advertising.

American media's stress on reaching young people is not new. Advertisers prefer to reach the young, whom they regard as better prospects for new products and for switching their brand loyalty. This is particularly obvious in the music and video markets.

> "Stop advertising gang materials." *(Kent, 15, Urban)*

> "Don't advertise tobacco, guns, sex, violence, drugs. . . . And don't glorify gangs." *(Dana, 16, Rural)*

The influence of television entertainment programming has a substantial impact on today's youths. Television executives regularly insist that their programming has no power whatsoever to influence the public, yet this position contradicts the most basic assumption in their industry. Commercial television is based entirely on the premise that broadcast advertising can alter the buying behavior of a significant segment of the huge viewing audience. So if television does not help shape viewers' attitudes—especially those of young people—then it should refund its massive revenues to the advertisers. After all, this would mean that the advertisers are being misled into believing that the medium can shape viewers' attitudes.

Other media professionals realize that their audiences, especially younger viewers, are starting to develop more savvy than ever before.

> "We know today's kids and young adults have a greater level of sophistication when viewing television. They've already seen more television than their parents ever expected to see. They want to learn more about the world and themselves. Our goal is to respond by delivering accurate news shows and thought-provoking programs." *(Judy, 39, Television Program Director)*

Indeed, young people do understand, and often challenge, programming decisions.

> "They should put TV shows on about gangs and effects of joining." *(Trey, 18, Inner City)*

> "Show gang prevention programs." *(Andy, 17, Suburban)*

> "Portray more TV shows where kids are faced with the decision to join gangs and decide not to." *(Beth, 15, Urban)*

> "Promote *good* things that happen with kids and show how much fun gang-free life is." *(John, 16, Rural)*

> "Have a gang conference over the television. Have movies about how much hurt people go through when a family or friends are

involved in gangs. How can we stop gangs if kids think they're okay?" *(Elia, 17, Inner City)*

"Do not promote gangs in entertainment. Movies make gangs seem 'cool.' This is so fake!" *(Chanel, 16, Suburban)*

"Put age limits or warnings on certain tapes, movies, and television shows like they do on smokes and alcohol." *(Tina, 17, Suburban)*

News

In the media, *news*, like entertainment, is a profit-oriented business. The news media are concerned with maximizing their advertising revenues, which requires them to tinker endlessly with both the format and substance of their news programs, with the goal of attracting the largest, most affluent audience possible.

Of course, we must remember that what the public wants is not necessarily what it needs—and what the media report is not necessarily proportionate to what is happening. When profit-oriented media organizations must choose between giving their audiences what they want or giving them what they need, the media usually prefer to please their audiences . . . even when this might be misleading or disproportionate coverage. Interestingly, fifty-five percent of the youths surveyed said that they would prefer the media to report "more about the positive activities and accomplishments of youths."

"Cover more of the good things that kids do, not just the bad. This only makes kids want to do the bad stuff more because it gets attention." *(Maggie, 16, Urban)*

"Do not exploit gang members as heroes or make stars of them. Tell the truth about what they are: heartless, cruel, unlawful." *(Karen, 17, Urban)*

To keep their audiences, the media often ask as little as possible from them. Media decision makers usually opt for simple, exciting, and entertaining reporting rather than complex, enlightening, and challenging coverage.

News coverage has the ability to create relationships quickly and intimately. The very nature of the small screen prompts news deliverers to utilize more close-ups to transmit the message. These close-ups reflect the personal and social contact that is characteristic of television. Television simulates intimate relationships between total strangers by bringing viewers close to actors and reporters. We allow these strangers to come into our homes on a regular basis; they become our friends.

Camera angles, special effects, editing, and live or taped reporting also influence the relationship between the coverage and the viewer. However, few factors have more impact than the anchorpersons and on-air reporters. In the process of reporting, newspersons legitimize certain stories. Viewers, especially young people, think of these television personalities as being important by the very nature of their being on television. Like media technology, television anchorpersons are important to the process by which television news is made credible, as well as its success in dramatizing and sensationalizing the news.

What influences the accuracy of reporting? Deadlines certainly affect how and how well stories are reported. Even more pressure, however, comes from the competitive nature of the media. Each reporter from each medium is driven to outreport the others. Sometimes this results in inaccurate, incomplete, and biased coverage—to get the story to the public before anyone else does. Many experts claim that television has a responsibility to do more—to be complete in what it reports. This means that when television portrays visually disturbing crimes, it must also report the consequences of those crimes. Most youths surveyed want television news coverage to be more balanced.

> "Report what happens to kids who are heavily involved in gangs. And pay more positive attention to the kids who aren't in gangs." *(Jennifer, 16, Rural)*

> "Show undercover reports of dangers of gang involvement. Report stories on how many deaths occur." *(Maria, 15, Urban)*

> "Focus more on the positive and less on the negative. When other groups of young people show leadership, report that." *(Marianne, 17, Urban)*

Many teens want television news to avoid reporting anything at all about gangs.

"Don't publicize incidents that involve gangs. Why give them that kind of attention?" *(Lucas, 15, Rural)*

"Television shouldn't give in to gangs by reporting everything they do. Gangs like that kind of attention." *(Pete, 16, Inner City)*

"Quit giving so much coverage and front-page headlines to gangs. People start to think that you get famous for doing bad things if they are on the front page. Put good news on the front page." *(Tonya, 17, Rural)*

"Don't promote gang involvement by giving air time or recognizing specific groups." *(Lou, 18, Inner City)*

"Reporting gang activities is the major fuel behind their actions. Even though good for ratings, this kind of news is detrimental to viewers and the entire community." *(Zach, 17, Urban)*

Though electronic reporting has the ability to reach audiences more quickly, this benefit also has disadvantages. It limits, or discourages, coverage in places where the camera cannot travel. This can result in no coverage at all of an otherwise important story. Because broadcast reporting often serves breaking stories with live coverage, this also limits the reporter in rechecking details. In contrast, print reporters usually have more time to check out a story and provide complete, accurate coverage.

Because broadcast news is presented within a strict time frame, the length of time it devotes to each story is substantially limited. Sound bites and video bites, instead of in-depth analyses, drive messages home to the audience. A complementary method for news and public affairs issues to be presented in a more complete way is through public-service programs and announcements.

"Have a lot of anti-gang public-service announcements. Air them all the time." *(Sarah, 16, Suburban)*

"Don't glorify gangs. Make anti-gang public-service announcements." *(Cheryl, 15, Urban)*

"Get involved with promoting non-gang activities." *(Raylene, 17, Inner City)*

"Have a message that violence is bad, along with smoking, guns. . . ." *(Dana, 16, Rural)*

One of the most significant ways the mass media influence audiences is through ideology. Simply, they use their media, intentionally or unintentionally, to impress their own ideas on the public. These positions often exclude the interests of some groups and classes and certain races and religions. However, this does not mean that audiences have no power. Interested viewers can submit complaints to management, ask for editorial response time in the news, boycott stations and their advertisers, and take legal action. Hopefully, these information consumers will take the appropriate action that helps build positive change and inclusion into the media environment.

Untapped Potential

Considering everything said so far, I offer another perspective about television's influence. The mere counting of hours tells us almost nothing about television's relevance in our lives. Some things cannot be quantified, especially when we consider how television affects those who have grown up with it.

We tend to presume that television has captivated and controlled our nation, especially today's young people. This presumption, however, ignores the overwhelming realm of motivations and influences—beyond television— that plays upon our children. Whether measuring the level of social crises, gang-related crimes, or falling student test scores, we do not have proof that television is the original or sustaining culprit. However, there is no denying that the medium's influence is a potent one.

Of course, the ideal use of television involves educators who also immerse themselves in the medium to produce top-quality programming options. Teachers and students benefit from weaving public, commercial, cable, and satellite television programming into their lessons. By participating with their students in these viewing experiences, and critiquing style and substance, teachers can have a monumental impact in the education movement.

Television, as an educational medium, offers personal choices in other ways. It provides a form of literacy that is emerging from what used to be merely a passive experience. Television has become a hybrid—half video, half computer. This media mix creates unlimited opportunities for learning, interactivity, and personal choice.

From preschool through college, we recognize the impact of high technology in the learning process. This excites us, as we continue to redevelop our lesson plans to satisfy the natural and inspired curiosities of our students. *(Marge, 46, School Principal)*

YOUNG PEOPLE . . . RESPONSIBLE FOR THEMSELVES

Hopefully, viewers born in the 1970s, 1980s, and 1990s have emerged as the most knowledgeable and critical media watchers, maybe even cynical ones. Yes, they know how much network announcers get paid, the personal histories of sitcom producers, and the shake-up patterns for morning talk shows. They developed their critical eye in early childhood.

Taking Control

For many reasons, in spite of ongoing media attempts, young viewers are learning not to accept at face value what media moguls put in front of them. Just as earlier generations enjoyed the process of dissecting the newest mechanical devices—from erector sets to cars—young viewers are carefully examining commercials, cartoons, and prime-time movies. If bored with school or work or relationships, they turn to television. They have become the first masters of the remote control.

Hopefully our children are learning more about how television influences their thoughts and actions. In *Hollywood Versus America* (1992), Michael Medved analyzes the media, especially television, for an array of sins. Medved refers to media influences with chapter titles such as: "Promoting Promiscuity," "Encouraging Illegitimacy," "Maligning Marriage," "Urging to Offend," "The Infatuation with Foul Language," "The Addiction to Violence," "Hostility to Heroes," and "Bashing America." Many social scientists echo Medved's concerns, especially as they relate to violence. They say that violence is shown everywhere, justified, rewarded, socially accepted, clean, and considered inconsequential. Simply, the media are delivering violence as an effective solution to solving problems.

"Get away from glorification of violence." *(Russ, 18, Inner City)*

"Don't promote guns on TV shows." *(Moria, 16, Urban)*

"Show less violence because it begins to look glamorous." *(Tony, 17, Suburban)*

We do know that as more control rests within the hands of the viewer, the less that control will reside with the media producers, including advertisers. So how will this influence the ways in which our children view themselves? As they develop their own personal identities and self-perceptions, young people need to learn how to understand the difference between multidimensional images on the screen and reality. This is especially important for the people who have questionable self-esteem and vulnerabilities, including those who make the decision to join youth gangs.

Control—and for many, the perceived lack of it—has played an important part in the lives and choices of our young people. Far from opting to view passively, these audiences have preferred channel surfing and the dozens, if not hundreds, of options before them. *Impulse viewing* has become the norm: network television, cable movies, rented videos, interactive video games. For many youths who choose to immerse themselves in television, this device gives them a perverted sense of control—unfortunately, however, within the context of an unreal world.

Youths need to understand that interacting with images on a screen, however well simulated, does not represent real-life human experiences between people who share the same space at the same time. Yes, interactive technology continues to provide some tremendous opportunities for those who cannot be together. Young people must learn to distinguish, however, between the importance of staying in touch with reality and real relationships and responsibilities. Our children and teens must maintain balance between technological contact and human interaction.

Getting Past Materialism

Whatever transpires in the world of media, one pivotal factor will define success or failure in reaching our young people. This will necessitate our youths' distinguishing what role *materialism* plays in their own lives.

Human beings have always wanted and craved material things. As time has passed, this craving has grown even stronger, though some cultures do not measure themselves principally by the standard of comfort and safety in the material world. Unfortunately, America does.

Our children and teens live in what is considered an "affluent society." Put simply, we not only have significant material wealth; we also want this wealth more than we want most anything else! This arrangement of priorities has tested our civilization and stunted our value system.

Money serves as the driving force behind material wealth. This prompts confusion in our nation's youth, who have fewer opportunities to earn and save money, because it is less available to more of them. Today, money—and all the things it can buy—motivates young people, especially those in youth gangs. This obsession has created extraordinary pressures for those young people who cannot attain it legitimately, thus the appeal of crime for profit in the youth gang.

> "Someone needs to control advertising so that people are not so urged to consume material things. Desire for prestige and material things prompts young people to join gangs, because they feel they can't get them legitimately." *(Olivia, 21, Urban)*

Marketers, working through the media, need to remember that today's young people have grown out of a different history, with a different set of life experiences. They have learned to cope and to use new skills and a different set of expectations than their parents. Yet the pressures to succeed—and to have money to buy things—are just as profound today as ever before.

Chapter Highlights

- Since the 1990s, television programs have particularly reflected societal changes, such as shared parenting, single parenting, minority issues, social conflicts, and emotional challenges.
- Television has provided young people with newfound relationships, however fictionalized, as substitutes for getting to know one another in the flesh.
- Television offers a variety of gratifications. It invites viewers to relax, to disregard their real-life problems, to surrender themselves to attractive screen people, and to become absorbed in events.
- Many experts consider the *television habit* addictive, especially when viewers spend as much as forty percent of their free time in front of a television set.
- For young people, especially those in dysfunctional families, television often serves as the only nurturer and friend in the home, the only thing they can depend on.
- One simple but critical principle will continue to influence media decisions: profit.
- The power of the entertainment industry to influence the actions of others

emanates from its ability to redefine what constitutes normal behavior in this country.

- The American media appeal to their audiences through middle- and upper-class values by emphasizing personalities, personal celebrity, and individual achievement.

- Commercial television is based entirely on the premise that broadcast advertising can alter the buying behavior of a significant segment of the huge viewing audience.

- When profit-oriented media organizations must choose between giving their audiences what they want or giving them what they need, the media usually opt to please their audiences.

- News coverage has the ability to create relationships quickly and intimately. Television simulates intimate relationships between total strangers by bringing viewers close to actors and reporters.

- Both deadlines and competition between the various media are two major components affecting news coverage.

- One of the most significant ways the mass media influence audiences is through ideology. They use their media, intentionally or unintentionally, to impress their own ideas on the public, often excluding particular groups.

- The ideal use of public, commercial, cable, and satellite television involves educators who also immerse themselves in the medium to produce top-quality programming options.

- As more control rests within the hands of the viewer, the less that control will reside with the media producers, including advertisers.

- Interacting with images on a screen, however well simulated, does not represent real-life human experiences between people who share the same space at the same time.

Chapter 12

Partnerships

Little drops of kindness.
    They mean the world.
        To a hurt.
            And lost soul.

Sweet nothings of happiness,
    Whispered in the ear of anyone,
        Can warm
            Even the coldest of hearts.

A hug, an embracement of caring
    Dissolves all pain and anguish.
        Healing in an everlasting comfort,
        Healing in heart.

A gift without words.
    A touch.
        A look.
        A smile. . . .

A gift dear to any soul.
    A gift so precious.
        Give the gift
        Of eternal kindness.

Lily, 13, Inner City

As the children frolic by,
With energy to spare,
I begin to wonder why
I've contributed time and care.

I've given up my weekends
For youngsters in the sun.
And . . . hang time with the friends
So a few kids can have some fun.

Oh, the games haven't brought
Any Saturday morning freedom.
Yet, the values they have taught,
Nothing else could beat 'em.

Young players work together
And share what they know.
They encourage one another,
Long-term, it will show.

Through much time and effort,
These kids gain a lot.
But I also profit
Just to see the winning shot.

For all the kids I cheer!
Now they are more than names.
I am a proud volunteer
For the Inner City Games.

The giving of myself
Is, by far, the largest part.
Kindness is the wealth
The games have brought my heart.

Jennifer, 18, Urban

MOBILIZING COMMUNITIES

Resolving youth gang problems in a community takes planning. The basic
questions for planning should not be "How can we most efficiently get rid
of gang members in our community?" but "How can we integrate gang

members into a larger, legitimate, mainstream community?" and "How can we best put their intelligence, talents, and energies to work *for them* and *for the community?*"

For this to happen, necessary changes will need to occur across the community between the community and its children. The youth gang problem varies at different times and places. It can have a direct and an indirect impact. These issues must be handled on their own terms, as well as in relation to the other fundamental community problems.

Certainly, *community consciousness* is necessary to raise the general level of awareness within a defined area. In particular, local communities and governments can form alliances with the media to produce public-service campaigns to keep citizens informed, such as through public-service announcements, public-affairs programs, editorials, special events, and mentoring. They can have a more substantial role in working with the media to address youth gang issues in news and local programming. Everyone needs to work together to make a commitment to raise community awareness about the issues and to increase knowledge, change attitudes, and motivate citizens to participate in change.

CREATING PARTNERSHIPS

Strategies that have a positive impact on gang prevention and intervention will also effect crime, mental illness, homelessness, truancy, and other forms of social discord.

No effort at restoring order in the community will work without a full partnership between local citizens and local agencies, especially law enforcement and schools, to affect what is happening in the community. These *community partnerships*, such as those with the media, must involve everyone in the community. They need to represent all racial, ethnic, religious, and economic groups, and they must provide a foundation for restoring order.

Simply, community partnerships instill *ownership* in those who live in, and are affected by, their communities. This includes facing problems and finding solutions, including youth gangs. In a community partnership, each citizen's role does not end when order is restored. The responsibility continues with maintaining order and preventing future disorder.

Policy partnerships take community partnerships to the next level. Arnold P. Goldstein and C. Ronald Huff, editors of *The Gang Intervention Handbook* (1993), discuss the importance of policy partnerships. These collaborations require close cooperation among government agencies at all levels, as well as private-sector participation involving for-profit and nonprofit organizations. To succeed, policy partnerships must address the following:

- Mandatory preschool development programs.
- Programs targeting youth service and youth employment.
- A full-employment economy.
- Targeted, community-based, public-private (nonprofit) intervention programs in high-risk urban areas.

Mandatory Preschool Development Programs

Working with children before they enter kindergarten can have a critical impact on childhood development. Programs such as Head Start help prepare children to succeed in school. A mandatory program also would help reduce child abuse, because younger children are in school part of the day. Historically, these programs relieve stress for the family caregiver and improve the child's daily nutrition.

Amazing new knowledge is now available about brain development in children from birth to age three. A mandatory program for those ages three and older would help develop cognitive and social skills, including conflict resolution and anger management, at an early age.

Preschool programs are profitable for everyone. Research confirms that Head Start children are more productive later in life as well. A substantial majority of them graduate from high school, and most go on to postsecondary education. According to 1990 findings by the Eisenhower Foundation, for every $1.00 spent on early prevention and intervention, taxpayers save $4.75 in remedial education, welfare, and crime later on.

Programs Targeting Youth Service and Youth Employment

According to research, the population most vulnerable to youth gang involvement is fourteen-to-twenty-four year-old males, especially those living in poor, inner-city neighborhoods.

For at-risk youths who are not employed or in school, one possible training alternative is a national *youth service*. This would involve the youths— ages fourteen to twenty-one—in service projects such as conservation programs or job-training corps to help them develop skills while serving their country. Following the service, the youth would be guaranteed at least one year of employment in the private sector, the government, or the military.

"If we had somewhere to go to learn a skill or a trade, then we would have some kind of choice about our own futures." *(Tenaya, 14, Inner City)*

"If the government trained me, I'd be willing to work for them to pay them back for having faith in me." *(Klein, 15, Urban)*

A Full-Employment Economy

Gang members often quit high school in rebellion, or they leave because of disciplinary measures, academic failure, and/or the failure of an unresponsive educational system. At one time, these dropouts could find decent jobs without a high school diploma. Hard labor in manufacturing plants produced a lucrative wage. Today, however, many of these industrial and manufacturing jobs are gone. Ours is a service-based economy. So what is left?

To many, gang membership is the only alternative. The gang provides activity and income. To the gang member, drug trafficking and other illegal enterprises are equal opportunity employers. These substitutes resolve the hardship created by employment that mandates minimum or maximum levels of education and specific job skills. However, many gang members would prefer decent paying jobs to the gang life, but they lack the skills and the attitudes to obtain and hold them.

"Help kids find a good job so they don't go to gangs for one of the things kids go to them for . . . money." *(Russell, 17, Urban)*

"Pay workers more so poverty is not such a problem. Where appropriate, give jobs to kids between fourteen and eighteen years old." *(Olivia, 21, Urban)*

"Make young people feel good about working instead of useless." *(Leo, 17, Suburban)*

"Nobody wants to work for minimum wage. That's why they turn to selling dope." *(Zannie, 17, Inner City)*

Youths have diverse feelings about the employment of gang members.

"Make sure they have no employees in gangs." *(Jennifer, 16, Rural)*

"Hire more people who have interacted with gangs." *(Westley, 16, Inner City)*

"Keep the youths employed and work them longer hours." *(Dan, 16, Inner City)*

"Offer jobs to youth gangsters who want out of their gangs." *(Maria, 15, Urban)*

"Give opportunities for past gang members to change their lives through employment." *(Felix, 16, Suburban)*

Unemployment and underemployment have a disproportionate impact on minorities, especially in the inner city—the people who are most vulnerable to joining gangs. It is obvious that these youths must have extraordinary internal values and external support to resist the lure of gangs and their illegal activities.

"Business owners should not be afraid of kids because they are not all bad. There are a lot of talented kids out there." *(Nereyda, 17, Urban)*

"Offer incentives for children who quit gangs." *(Maggie, 16, Urban)*

The youths surveyed suggested creative ways for businesses to help establish gang-free communities.

"Contribute money and resources to community organizations that work hard dealing with youth gangs in the communities where the businesses are run. Openly and willingly support community organizations and individuals who are helping these youth gang members come away from their gangs." *(Zach, 17, Urban)*

"Sponsor events or activities to prevent kids from joining gangs." *(Beth, 15, Urban)*

"Help buy guns back from gang members." *(Ray, 17, Urban)*

"Fund community projects." *(Russ, 18, Inner City)*

"Donate money for billboards, commercials, public-service announcements, and whatever else will reach kids to discourage them from joining gangs." *(Cheryl, 15, Urban)*

To help with the external support, it is important for communities to make a strong commitment to full employment for all those of working age who can, and want to, work. To accomplish this, still more policy partnerships need to be formed and fortified with resources. This means a strong dedication to getting these youths trained and placed in jobs. This would also include on-the-job training and working with youth apprentices. In reality, when gang members have full-time employment, they have less time to hang out with their gangs and get into trouble.

"Keeping a youth employed and giving him lots of work will help keep him out of gang involvement." *(Dan, 16, Inner City)*

"Offer jobs to teens. This takes away time for them to be on the streets." *(Jodi, 17, Urban)*

For those of us who work with juvenile justice issues, the rationale to support this is simple: We pay now by creating and providing jobs, or we pay later with additional social services and prisons.

Targeted, Community-Based Programs

Communities need to offer both broad-based and narrowly focused programs to assist youths with their non-entry into—or exit from—gangs. Several of the many possible services might include:

Counseling and support services. We know that dysfunctional families have a much higher percentage of children who join gangs. Counseling can help families communicate with each other and begin to heal.

Home visits. Research bears out the value of programs that include home visits by social service professionals with at-risk families. Regular contact with these professionals helps families reduce the frequency of child abuse and neglect, the length of time on welfare, and the level and frequency of crimes committed by the children.

Adult mentoring. According to the Office of Juvenile Justice (*Juvenile Justice Bulletin*, April 1997), *mentoring* programs for disadvantaged children and teenagers have proven a promising approach to enriching children's lives. They address the child's need for positive adult contact, as well as provide one-on-one support and advocacy for the needy child. Mentoring is also a great way for community volunteers to address the problems created by family dysfunction, socioeconomics, and racial/ethnic challenges.

Youth centers. These facilities provide a physical alternative to hanging out on the streets. They often serve as neutral zones—places where kids can find refuge from dangerous neighborhoods and the gang environment. These programs need to help youths feel good about themselves.

"Show teens you trust them." *(Kristina, 17, Urban)*

"Involve teens in volunteer programs to show them they are needed." *(Marisela, 16, Rural)*

When possible, youth centers should offer a variety of recreational activities, especially those that reinforce a positive group or team experience, such as basketball, bowling, movie nights, and athletic contests. Also, centers should offer special programs to help youths with difficult choices, such as gang mediation and awareness programs, prenatal counseling, parent effectiveness training, and anger management and conflict resolution classes.

"Sponsor programs targeted to keeping kids out of trouble." *(Felix, 16, Suburban)*

"Offer youth involvement with service projects." *(Jodi, 17, Urban)*

"Sponsor programs and projects that encourage kids to get involved in everything from art classes to sports to chess." *(Maggie, 16, Urban)*

"Have places for kids to go if they are in a bad home." *(Russ, 18, Inner City)*

"Start building more boys and girls clubs so kids have a place to go to get off the streets." *(Arnoldo, 16, Inner City)*

Graffiti removal. Removing graffiti from buildings and other structures sends a message to youth gangs that they are unwelcome. Removal is a nuisance to gangs, which use graffiti to communicate. One caution: graffiti removers are often at risk for retaliation from the graffiti gang.

> "Set up weekly white-washes or painting at gang-affiliated locations, like walls, benches, and buildings." *(Jodi, 17, Urban)*

> "Have neighborhood watch programs to look out for spray paintings and other graffiti." *(Cassandra, 15, Urban)*

Tattoo removal. Medical facilities in many communities offer free tattoo removal to those youths who want to exit their gangs. This is an important opportunity to offer support to youths who want a fresh start.

Neighborhood organizations. Neighbors must continue to work together, and with law enforcement and schools, to help eradicate youth gang activity. This is the best way to make a strong statement to youths, neighbors, and others—youth gangs included—that one is willing to take a stand to protect the best interests of one's family and community.

> "Offer counseling groups or discussion groups for children in gangs." *(Maggie, 16, Urban)*

> "Have evening activities and events that involve youths." *(Jodi, 17, Urban)*

> "Be there for troubled teens in the community. Act as another family-like group. Listen to them. Help resolve their troubled spirit and conscience. Establish a youth group that responds to youth gang members who want to get out. It should serve as both a peer group and a support group." *(Zach, 17, Urban)*

> "Youth outreach will help urge youths to examine their values and those of the gang. It will help them understand why gangs are so destructive." *(Olivia, 21, Urban)*

> "Provide support somewhere for these kids to talk and feel safe." *(Trent, 20, Rural)*

Neighborhood efforts require a substantial united commitment. Successful activities require participants to do the following:

- Report all gang activity and crimes.
- Organize neighborhood watches.
- Have a visible presence in the neighborhood.
- Help law enforcement learn where gang houses are so that the police can eliminate them.
- Organize for effectiveness and long-term commitment.

Town meetings. These help pull together neighborhood and community leaders, business representatives, social service providers, and affected families. In this forum, all parties can discuss and develop ways to involve all community resources to address the youth gang problems confronting them.

Faith organizations. One of the best resources for parents and families is faith organizations, including churches and religious institutions, many of which have taken an assertive role by organizing anti-gang programs for the neighborhood youths. These programs offer refuge, inclusion/belonging, support, esteem-building opportunities, discipline, and spiritual growth.

> "Hold mass or anti-gang services." *(Sean, 19, Urban)*

> "Teach kids not to join gangs and give them spiritual help to leave." *(Sarah, 16, Suburban)*

> "Go out into the community and preach to the people in the hood." *(Selena, 15, Suburban)*

Government. Often this serves as the official umbrella for community partnerships. It can be the most comprehensive or the most focused with its programs and offerings. Youths often turn to government first—and last—for help.

> "Put more money into building 'safe houses,' community shelters, and other places of refuge." *(Selena, 15, Suburban)*

> "Take troubled kids away from their families." *(Teresa, 15, Suburban)*

"Get harder on family abuse and desertion laws." *(Russ, 18, Inner City)*

"Protect children when they are young so that they grow up in stable and healthy environments." *(Marisela, 16, Rural)*

"Help needy families." *(Russell, 17, Urban)*

"Build more parks for kids to distract them from joining gangs." *(Christopher, 18, Urban)*

"Build treatment facilities, not prisons." *(Andy, 17, Suburban)*

"Create better security nets for poor families." *(Olivia, 21, Urban)*

"Stop worrying about other countries' problems and start dealing with our own." *(S.D., 16, Inner City)*

"Help kids understand that they really mean something to somebody and that they aren't just another Social Security number." *(Tonya, 17, Rural)*

Whatever the particular community's youth gang issues, nothing is more important than the mandate for partnered efforts. No one person, no one neighborhood, no one local government, and no one social service agency can do this alone. Total community involvement, through creative partnerships and ongoing collaboration, offers the needed force and support to resolve each community's youth gang challenges, one day at a time.

Chapter Highlights

- A critical focus for community partnerships is how we can integrate youth gang members into a larger, legitimate, mainstream community, and how we can best put their intelligence, talents, and energies to work *for them* and *for the community.*
- *Community partnerships* instill *ownership* in those who live in, and are affected by, their communities.
- In a community partnership, each citizen's role does not end when order

is restored. That responsibility continues with maintaining order and preventing future disorder.

- *Policy partnerships* take community partnerships to the next level by requiring close collaboration among governmental agencies at all levels. They also require involvement from the private sector through for-profits and nonprofits.

- Mandatory preschool programs—for those age three and older—help develop the child's thinking and social skills, including conflict resolution and anger management.

- For at-risk youths who are not employed or in school, a national *youth service* could provide valuable training and subsequent employment opportunities.

- Unemployment and underemployment have a disproportionate impact on minorities, especially in the inner city—the people who are most vulnerable to joining gangs.

- Communities need to make a strong commitment to full employment for all of those of working age who can—and want to—work.

- Communities need to offer both broad-based and narrowly focused programs to assist youths with their non-entry into—or exit from—gangs, for example:

—Counseling and support services.

—Home visits.

—Adult mentoring.

—Youth centers.

—Graffiti removal.

—Tattoo removal.

—Neighborhood organizations.

—Faith support.

—Town meetings.

- Total community involvement, through creative partnerships and ongoing collaboration, offer the needed force and support to resolve each community's youth gang challenges, one day at a time.

Part IV

Family and Child

Chapter 13

Families

Respect is a young child's image of a hard-working parent. The toddler esteems the parents who are going through tough times, but do not forget to love him. The parents are attempting to shelter the family and nurture their children. Respect is not traded for care, but it is given freely, in gratitude. As a result, respect is the silent appreciation for a job well done. *(John, 13, Suburban)*

Kindness is the way a mother wipes a tear from her child's eye. Tenderly, she wipes away the tears along with the pains or fears that may cause the child to weep. She gently caresses the child in so kind a way that the child is almost instantly comforted. The child will always feel that mother will bring comfort when he or she is upset, only because this is a small gesture of kindness. Truly, kindness is represented here and frequently people forget how this sort of thing affects how they think and feel. *(Gwendolyn, 13, Suburban)*

IT STARTS WITH THE FAMILY

Probably the most significant influences in the youth's development are family and friends. Of course, the family's role in helping develop the child is the first and, historically, the most influential. As children grow into adolescence and adulthood, however, often the family is replaced, or at least rivaled, by peer groups.

Parents have never been so stretched in the demands for their time and presence. Work, family, and many other commitments take claim of their time and energies. Though they are spending less time with their children, most parents are working to help their offspring adjust to these demands. This parenting consciousness may never have had such a presence in this nation. Adults realize that parenthood is no longer based on economics or dependencies. For the first time in history, parenthood is optional.

Unfortunately, these same modern times impose stresses that many parents strive to overcome—pressures that directly impact their children, such as divorce. About one-half of today's marriages will end in divorce. Millions of the children of divorce are adolescents. At least twenty-five percent of today's children will live with a stepparent before reaching age sixteen; one-third will live in single-parent families, usually with the mother as head of the household.

Broken families, blended families, single-parent families, and joint-custody families create challenges for both fathers and mothers. These parents can generally look to their own parents for positive parental role modeling, with family as a center of focus. However, today's parents often have no one to teach them about part-time parenting.

> "These are tough times. So, I adjust my thinking to help her as she changes and grows rapidly through this transition to adulthood." *(Barbara, mother of Mary, 16, Suburban)*

> "Because ours is a broken family, I recognize the importance of just 'being there' to support and encourage her choices to be a responsible adult." *(Sandy, mother of Jasmine, 16, Urban)*

In addition to the stresses of changed families, parents and their children will probably undergo economic changes. Sometimes teens must take on jobs to assist their families, or their families move to new homes and neighborhoods. These demands produce upheavals in the family when adolescents are already struggling with internal and external dilemmas that accompany their adolescent revolution.

For families in which remarriage occurs, children also must learn the identities of stepparents, and stepsiblings. At the very least, this produces awesome expectations. Equally significant, as these children are learning their new "roles," so are their stepparents. One important rule can help stepparents ease part of the stress: Stepparents are not replacements . . . they are additions. Of course, not all single parents remarry.

More adults are choosing to live together. Though this is a less formal legal commitment, all the complications, expectations, pressures, and frustrations often equal or surpass those of a marriage. This can compound the confusion and insecurities of emerging adults.

Parents and caregivers are struggling to survive these many, intertwining strains. When they cannot overcome difficulties, many lose control and turn to "outside sources"—often engaging in substance abuse—to ease their woes and soothe their pain. More than ever, parents need to provide support to their teens during these transitions. Unfortunately, too many of these parents are struggling to support themselves.

THE ROLE OF THE PARENT

As teenagers progress through adolescence, one of their major adjustments involves *authority*. To understand the impact of authority, they need to discern the role that parents and other adults play in their lives.

Setting Limits, Establishing Rules

By setting rules for children during early childhood, and living by them, families learn what to expect from each other. Rules also help young people understand what they can expect from their group identities. They learn how to adapt what they learn in their families to their new "families" outside the home.

Rules should not pit parents against teens. Family rules should not give adolescents the impression that they were created solely to cause trouble and frustration. At the same time, parents must remember that certain rules are crucial to the safety and well-being of their teens, no matter how loud the protests.

Parents also need to realize that their teens are living by rules established by others as well. Teachers and administrators set up guidelines for school attendance and mandated behavior on school grounds. Employers define work rules and expectations. Peer groups determine their own friendship rules and regulations. Then, of course, there is the rest of the world.

Parents need to believe in their adolescents to prioritize the rules in their own lives. These same teenagers will probably struggle to understand which rules supersede others, but this stimulates a viable part of the growth-and-choice aspect of their lives.

"I expect my kids to be honest and respectful of others. I want them to follow a few basic rules we have in the house, and strive to achieve a happy life." *(Steven, father of Amaris, 15, Suburban)*

"I hope for creative and healthy activities in safe environments, and expect them to take their good sense and judgment with them. They know their curfew. They know not to get isolated from the crowd. They know not to indulge in drugs, sex, and alcohol." *(Sandra, mother of Amber, 14, Urban)*

Parents and teens should focus their attention on a few workable guidelines for these rules.

Rules should be designed in positive ways, with clear expectations. They should keep the best interests of the most people in mind. This starts with meeting basic needs that focus on physical and emotional considerations.

Parents need to encourage their teens to be accountable for their own behaviors. They need to grow responsibly with their parents' rules. To reach self-empowerment, teens need to take care of themselves physically, mentally, emotionally, and spiritually. Adolescents must learn how to take care of their own needs first, before they can help their friends and their group. In contrast to "wants," youths' "needs" are those parts of their lives that they cannot exist without, even for a short time. First things first.

Testing rules will expose teenagers to new consequences. As they expand their roles in rule setting, teenagers also learn about new outcomes for expected behaviors. In addition, they expose themselves to new consequences for mishandled behaviors.

When teenagers take risks, they learn to appreciate the value of rules. Understanding why certain rules are required, adolescents learn the values of these dictates. When experimenting beyond known rules can reap better ones, both parents and teens should collaborate on new rules. Together, parents and teens should always remember the benefits as well as the potential consequences when crafting new rules.

Parents should correct their children in private. When problems arise, parents should deal with them in private rather than in front of their offsprings' peers, siblings, or other adults. This helps their children preserve their dignity and, therefore, encourages a more likely correction.

Perspective

To succeed in their authority, parents should help their children learn how to adapt their own thinking and values to daily living. This helps young people learn how to mature into adult decision makers, with the ability to live by their own decisions.

As youths get older, they tend to have a better understanding of what parents and other people of authority expect of them. In healthy environments, they learn how to adapt their own behaviors with what is "socially and legally acceptable." For some, this helps them carve out their identities and independence. For others, it produces a high level of frustration and often compliance with those—often, youth gangs—who lead them into socially unacceptable or illegal behavior.

Discipline

When having to address negative behavior, it is important for parents to remember that it is the present situation they need to address. Parents need to focus on what their children can do *now* to repair what has been done. They *cannot* undo the past. They *can* move forward with corrective action.

Also, to aid youths with these issues, parents and caregivers should help them determine whose issue it really is. Whoever is responsible for the situation needs to take *ownership* of it.

Thus, in dealing with their children's negative behaviors, parents do have options. One option is to *ignore* negative behavior and hope that it will go away.

A second option involves disciplining offspring through *intervention*. This style of discipline allows parents to step in to provide for the needs of their child, and to guide, teach, direct, and correct the behavior of the child. This requires parents to establish and enforce rules for socially acceptable behavior.

Often parents rely on discipline—even punishment—as a primary source of "teaching lessons" to their children who exhibit negative behavior. With this approach, parents should remember to "connect" the act of discipline with the negative behavior. When parents use such expressions as "You are being punished for your own good," teenagers struggle to understand what negative behavior prompted this response. Young people need to see the connection between the behavior and the consequence. For example, a teenage girl who takes her sibling's CD player without asking might be disciplined by having to give up her own player for a week. By making this connection between the inappropriate activity and the parental response, the teenager learns that consequences follow prohibited behaviors.

Parents have other alternatives as well. Through *interaction*, parents help their children solve problems. Both parents and their children work together to resolve issues and find appropriate behaviors. For example, parents can sit down with their teenager on report card day. They can talk about the grades and discuss possible ways for the teenager to pull up less than satisfactory grades. Parents should let their children, especially their teenagers, offer most of the suggestions, because they will have to deliver the solutions for improvement.

Parents—through *non-intervention*—can give emerging adults opportunities for "taking responsibility" for their actions and offering their own *corrective action*. For example, when a teenage son brings home the car dirtier than when he left with it, parents need to acknowledge this. Then they can ask him how he plans to correct this. The parents should let their son suggest the alternative, maybe by offering to wash the car on Saturday. This gives the teenager a chance to make amends and to feel good about finding solutions and acting upon them.

Other alternatives to punishment involve various forms of discipline. Parents can do the following:

- Express strong disapproval through candid communication.
- State their expectations in advance of—and following—the behavior.
- Give the youth choices for behavior and information about the rewards or consequences of each choice.
- Take action, but not punitive action.
- Allow the young person to experience the consequences of the negative behavior.
- Catch their child "doing something good" and reward him or her for this positive behavior.

When parents consider these alternatives, they can make tremendous strides. Discipline provides education. It helps parents direct their children and lay the foundation for their kids to develop internal self-control, self-direction, and efficiency.

Praise and Reward: Sound Alternatives

Unfortunately, too many parents focus their attention on what their children are failing to do, what rules they are breaking, and how they are not meeting society's standards of performance. This is unfortunate. It means that they ignore a vast majority of today's youths—those who *do* live by the rules, take responsibility for their actions, and make positive contributions to themselves and others.

Praise, therefore, works as a viable alternative. This gives parents ways to reconsider their relationship options. Praise empowers parents to *affirm* behavior when it produces positive results. Of course, praise needs to be appropriate to the action and the child's level of ability and accomplishment. Parents need to remember, too, that in all situations—whatever the level of success or failure—their offspring will usually look to them as an ongoing resource for love, appreciation, and acceptance.

Praise, like criticism, can be destructive, especially when parents use absolute language such as "always" and "never." These words place too much pressure on young people. They create too much anxiety and make future behavior too difficult to handle.

Praise should also describe the act or behavior. It should not include descriptions of personality or character. By praising personality traits, parents again place an excessive burden on their children. For example, saying "You always perform your best in school" can be too much to handle for a son who might bring home a B on his next report card.

In praising their children for action, parents must be careful not to use the praise as a put-down for a past action that did not succeed. They should focus on the child's present strength and accomplishment.

Young people need praise that helps them accept their accomplishments because of their successful efforts, not merely because they have met parental expectations. Parents need to augment their usual "I'm so proud of you for . . ." statements. When they enhance these messages with "You should feel very proud of yourself for . . . ," parents help their children empower themselves to feel pride in themselves for their own actions. This distinction encourages young people to do well, not to perform primarily to please someone else.

Parents have a responsibility to measure their offspring's successes. They should accept their children's mistakes as an important stage of learning. They also need to encourage their children to apply these mistake-lessons to the eventual successes they will experience.

How does the use of praise influence youths in their group settings? When young people feel good about themselves, they will generally transfer this high self-esteem to their relationships with others. Often they will excel as performers within the group, because they do not feel threatened by their own abilities or by the outcomes of their efforts.

"Having friends—and being part of my group—gives me both the recognition and understanding that I need when I do something extra for myself and others." *(LiAn, 16, Urban)*

"It is hard to stand alone. There is strength in numbers." *(Kristy, 17, Suburban)*

"My friends give me a sense of accomplishment, getting somewhere, being somewhere, being someone, having something someone else wants." *(Lisa, 16, Urban)*

FAMILIES RECLAIMING THEIR CHILDREN FROM GANGS

One of the most difficult challenges confronting today's families is the influence of youth gangs in their children's lives. As youth gangs grow in presence and dominance, it is now more important than ever for families—especially parents—to get involved in reclaiming their children.

The Youth Gang as "Family"

Many presumptions are floating around that assert that youths involved with gangs do not care about their own biological families. In most situations, this is far from true. In fact, for many youth gangsters, it is the threat of violence to their families—from their gang and others—that prompts them to join the gang in the first place.

Many gang members conceal their membership from their parents because they say it is "easier" on their mothers. They believe that this concealment will keep their moms from worrying about them. As for the parents, many of them deny their child's involvement in a gang, preferring to believe that the child is just mixed up with the wrong crowd.

Scott H. Decker and Barrik Van Winkle, in *Life in the Gang: Family, Friends and Violence* (1996), measure the relative importance of the gang and the family by asking youth gang members to choose between them. In a study they conducted among gang members, youths turned to their gangs to provide them with things like money and support for involvement in crime. This influence coincides with the youth's natural distancing from family that occurs during adolescence. It is compounded, however, by the extraordinary influence and authority that the gang asserts with negative, and illegal, behaviors.

However, in that same study, eighty-nine percent of those responding said that if forced to choose, they would select their biological family over their gang. The two most frequent reasons for this choice were (1) "The family cares for me more" and (2) "Blood relations are more important than gang affiliations."

When youths are forced to choose between their gangs and their families, something significant takes place. They must weigh competing values in their lives. For most members, gang life provides a place to find protection, companionship, and understanding. Their families, however, represent something even deeper: a commitment, with history—birth, nurturing, caring, support, and love—that surpasses what they have with their gang. Most gang members concede that the family attributes associated with gangs—caring, understanding, and financial support—do not run the depth of commitment that the biological family offers.

One compelling statistic from the Decker and Van Winkle study indicates that ninety-eight percent of youths currently involved in gangs would not want their son or daughter to join one. Most of these respondents described the violence associated with gang membership as a reason to keep their child from joining a gang.

Levels of Parental Involvement

For some parents, the awareness that their child is a gang member produces a natural feeling of anger and even jealousy directed toward the gang. They feel that the gang has taken their child away from them. Parental responses to their child's youth gang involvement vary.

Some parents—*family-first* parents—immerse themselves in an effort to assist their child and to restore the family. Putting the child and the situation first is a healthy way to address the youth gang problem.

Others—*rescuers*—commit themselves to a mission of saving their child while at the same time, minimizing their own fear and accountability. In the short term, the rescue mode can help the child because it involves family support, which also helps the parents through the adjustment process.

Crusaders—those who consider the project to save their children an obsession—often attempt to save other youths as well. While attempting to save everyone, these parents often suppress the root issues with their own children.

Still others—*negators*—know that they themselves have contributed to their child's joining a gang. They tend to respond more negatively. Their common responses include denial that the child is in trouble and denial of responsibility for the child's poor social, emotional, and spiritual well-being. Or, negators might accept the reality of the situation and be unwilling to help the child.

At the extreme are *detached* parents—those who just do not care. These parents refuse to participate in any opportunity to disengage their children from youth gangs.

Whatever the parents believe—and commit to—in attempting to disengage their children from gangs, the process can be more than difficult. Sometimes disengagement requires extreme measures, such as moving away.

> "Move when it starts or don't let them dress in gang colors or hang out with that group." *(Raylene, 17, Inner City)*

> "Move away from gangs!" *(Westley, 16, Inner City)*

> "Move away . . . now." *(Alisa, 16, Suburban)*

> "Love your kids enough to talk to them about getting out. If your child agrees to leave the gang, then be ready to move so that nothing bad will happen to that child or your family. Retaliation." *(Chanel, 16, Suburban)*

Parents of youth gang members share the frustrations of dealing with gang membership and how this involvement negatively affects family relationships. In contrast, a majority of gang members themselves will say that their gang involvement does not affect their biological families.

> "Make them choose between gang and family. If they choose the gang, then move them out—and far away from—the neighborhood." *(Jackie, 16, Urban)*

Looking for the Signs

No matter how difficult it is, parents and families need to face the reality that gangs are here to stay. Denying this fact would serve no one, especially those children who are vulnerable to joining them. To help reclaim their children or, hopefully, to prevent them from joining gangs, parents need to pay attention to the following signs:

- *Clothes.* Does the child have many clothes of the same color, or certain color combinations, such as black and blue or black and gold? This may indicate gang interest or involvement.

- *Jewelry.* Does the child wear a lot of gold jewelry? Is this jewelry similar to that worn by gangs? How did the child purchase it? Where did that money come from?

- *Money.* Does the child have large—and unaccounted for—amounts of money?

- *Pagers and portable phones.* Does the child really need to have a pager or phone? Does the child use it excessively and privately, especially in places and at times when normal social calls would not occur?

- *Gang symbols.* Does the child have gang symbols on schoolbooks, notebooks, clothes, and/or tattoos?

- *Language.* Does the child use special language, slang, or gang jargon to communicate?

- *Attitude.* Does the child exhibit an unfamiliar, an inappropriate, and a negative attitude about things at home, school, and elsewhere?

- *School performance and attendance.* Is the child's school performance sliding for no obvious reason? Has the child been repeatedly truant? Does the child violate curfew laws?

- *Friends.* Does the child "hang out" with people who all wear the same gang-related colors, speak in gang jargon, use gang signs, listen to the same distressful or violent music, carry weapons, get into trouble with the law, and engage in other irresponsible behavior?

Making a Commitment to the Kids

Certainly it is not just parents and families who want gang-free communities. However, families have the most to lose when gangs do claim their children. To help save their children from youth gangs, parents must make a commitment to their kids. I recommend that you, the parent, do as much as possible of the following, and the more, the better.

Serve as a positive role model. Know that your child watches what you say and do. You are often the first person your child models. Remember how important this can be, and make the best of it.

"Set good examples and urge kids into healthier fun and entertainment." *(Karen, 17, Urban)*

Get involved in your child's life . . . completely. Many children have excessive amounts of unstructured, unsupervised time. When possible, participate in positive activities with your child. Attend school functions. And show interest in your child's life by asking questions such as: Where are you going? When will you be home? Who are you going with? What's your favorite music group? What do you know about gangs? Do you know how much we love you and need you in this family? One caution: ask in a style that does not sound like an interrogation. Reassure your child that your home is their home.

"Learn more about the people your kids hang around with." *(Laquitta, 17, Urban)*

"Parental involvement is a must. Also, discipline. Instill values that reject the gang lifestyle. Forbid them from associating with known gang members." *(Olivia, 21, Urban)*

"Pay more attention to what youths are interested in." *(Answar, 17, Inner City)*

"Accept them as family members, no matter what." *(Maria, 15, Urban)*

"Always make your kids feel welcome at home." *(Ray, 17, Urban)*

"Give them a loving and caring environment." *(Lucas, 15, Rural)*

"Put the child in a safe home environment. Let her know that she means more than anything or anyone else in the world." *(Selena, 15, Suburban)*

"Give them what they need at home so they don't have to look for love somewhere else." *(Shawna, 17, Rural)*

Monitor your child's progress in school. Repeated truancy makes your child vulnerable to gang recruitment and peer pressure. Check with school attendance officers periodically to ensure that your child is attending school. Encourage your child's commitment to school and offer assistance with projects and homework.

> "Teach kids about peer pressure and show them that others—besides kids who will get them into trouble—do care for them. The family." *(Jackie, 16, Urban)*

> "My mom makes sure I go to school, bring my homework home, and do it. She always helps me when I have trouble with my assignments, and everything else." *(Nicole, 12, Suburban)*

Create positive, family-based alternatives. Organize and implement weekend activities with the family. Find ways to involve members more often. When planning, include suggestions from the child/children you are trying to protect from youth gangs.

> "Spend more time together as a family. Plan special nights to be together as a family." *(Christopher, 18, Urban)*

> "Do family stuff together to build a sense of belonging." *(David, 16, Suburban)*

> "Keep kids very involved. Do anything you can to keep them from roaming the streets." *(Jennifer, 16, Rural)*

> "Parents need to stay home more." *(Jimmy, 16, Suburban)*

Communicate with other parents. Build parental networks that help you help each other. When you share ideas with other parents, you can work collectively and creatively to resolve many issues. This can also help build a friendship network for your child.

> "My mother knows my friends and their parents. She cares enough to want to get involved with them too." *(Lyle, 13, Inner City)*

"I know I can go to my friend's house and be safe. My parents know that too." *(Suzanne, 17, Urban)*

"It makes me feel good that I matter enough to my family that they care who my friends are and what kinds of families they come from." *(Eric, 14, Suburban)*

Communicate openly and honestly with your child. More than *speaking at* your child, learn to *listen to* your child. *Really* listen. Be willing to listen to your child's concerns and to share yours. Even if your offspring has joined a gang, do everything possible to keep the lines of communication open. When you say something, mean it and follow through with what you promise, but do not promise more than you can deliver. In fact, underpromise and overdeliver, whenever possible. Work rigorously to establish and grow *trust* in the relationship with your child. Certainly love and support also have a critical place in relationship building between parents and their children.

"Trust more, talk more, be there, and care." *(Paul, 15, Inner City)*

"Parents need to pay more attention to their children and listen to them more." *(Zannie, 17, Inner City)*

"It's important for parents to tell their kids how much they want them out of their gang and how much it hurts to see them in one." *(Jon, 16, Inner City)*

"To parents I say: Show love and support by showing appreciation for family commitment and involvement." *(Marianne, 17, Urban)*

"It's as simple as 'be there,' especially when they are having rough times. Talk through arguments. Be more supportive about their choice of friends." *(Kristina, 17, Urban)*

"Parents need to show—and share—their feelings." *(Berra, 13, Urban)*

"For kids it means everything to know that they have a haven from a dangerous society. A place where they can talk about any problems, and someone will listen." *(Maria, 15, Urban)*

Other areas of necessary involvement are mentioned in detail throughout this book. They include, but are not limited to: participation in neighborhood watch programs, involvement with school and law enforcement programs and policies related to youth gangs, and interaction with community-wide youth programs and activities.

Expanding the Youth's Frame of Reference

Of all the hard lessons parents can teach their children, one of the hardest is a direct one: Face reality. How critical this lesson is in the life of a youth gangster. Part of this mandate requires that youths accept responsibility for their own behavior—for the choices they make.

Parents must learn how to distinguish between behavior and identity. This means that "what the child *does*" is not the same as "who the child *is*." Therefore, when the child performs poorly, parents must address the specific behavior, not attack the character of the child. The real identity of the child, therefore, is the "who" of that person, and not the "what" performed by the child.

When teaching children about choices, parents should teach them that life is filled with actions—and reactions. They have total control over how they react to things that happen to them. This is the part of their lives where they can make *real choices*. Knowing and taking advantage of this reality gives children genuine power and control over their lives to assert themselves in positive, productive ways.

Chapter Highlights

- The family's role in helping develop the child is the first and, historically, the most influential.

- Adults realize that parenthood is no longer based on economics or dependencies. For the first time in history, parenthood is optional.

- Contemporary families are undergoing diverse changes, from divorce to stepfamilies to live-in relationships. All of these non-traditional "families" add stress to the lives of parents and children.

- By setting rules for children during early childhood, and living by them, families learn what to expect from each other.
- Children live by rules established by others as well: teachers and administrators, employers, and friends.
- Parents and their offspring need to develop workable guidelines for their rules.

  —Rules should be designed in positive ways, with clear expectations.

  —Parents must encourage their children to be accountable for their own behaviors.

  —Testing rules will expose young people to new consequences.

  —When youths take risks, they learn to appreciate the value of rules.

  —Parents should correct their children in private.

- When addressing their children's negative behavior, parents need to focus on what their children can do *now* to repair what has been done.
- Youths need to take *ownership* for their actions and reactions.
- Parents have options when dealing with their child's negative behaviors. They can do the following:

  —Ignore the behavior and hope it will go away.

  —Punish the child without giving reasons.

  —Discipline the child through *intervention*, which allows the parents to provide for the needs of the child, to guide, teach, direct, and correct the child's behavior.

  —Resolve the behavior through *interaction*—a collaboration between parents and child to solve problems.

  —Give their child the opportunity to take responsibility through their own *non-intervention*.

- Too many parents focus their attention on what their children *fail* to do.
- *Praise* serves as a viable alternative in shaping a child's behavior. This gives parents ways to reconsider their relationship options.
- Young people need praise that helps them accept their accomplishments because of their own successful efforts, not merely because they have met parental expectations.
- Parents must accept their child's mistakes as an important stage of learning.

- Often, youths who feel good about their own accomplishments thrive in positive group settings because they do not feel threatened by their own abilities or the outcomes of their efforts.
- For many youth gangsters, it is the threat of violence to their families that prompts them to join gangs.
- When youths must make a choice between their gangs and their biological families, they must weigh competing values in their lives.
- The Decker and Van Winkle study indicates that nearly ninety percent of youth gang members, if forced to choose between their gangs and their families, would pick their biological families.
- Ninety-eight percent of gang members surveyed by Decker and Van Winkle would not want their own children to join gangs.
- Parental responses to their child's youth gang involvement vary:
  - *Family-first* parents immerse themselves in an effort to assist their child and to restore the family.
  - *Rescuers* commit themselves to a mission of saving their child, while minimizing their own responsibility in their child's decision to join a gang.
  - *Crusaders* try to save their own child and everyone else's, which helps them suppress the root causes for their own child's gang membership.
  - *Negators* know that they have contributed to their child's gang membership, but they tend to deny it.
  - *Detached* parents just do not care and refuse to participate.
- Parents need to pay attention to the following indicators and signs:
  - Clothes.
  - Jewelry.
  - Money.
  - Pagers and portable phones.
  - Gang symbols.
  - Language.
  - Attitude.
  - School performance and attendance.
  - Friends.
- To help their children make positive choices, parents need to do the following:

—Serve as positive role models.

—Get involved in their child's life . . . completely.

—Monitor their child's progress in school.

—Create positive, family-based alternatives.

—Communicate with other parents.

—Communicate openly, and often, with their own child.

- Teaching children that they have control over their own reactions and responses helps them learn the power of asserting themselves in positive, productive ways.

Chapter 14

Ultimately . . . The Youth's Choice

I will make it.
I will be somebody.
I will conquer my villains, bit by bit
To make it in this society.

Who am I?
I am an ordinary girl, I will not lie,
Trying to make it day by day in our world.
I think now, there is no time to be shy.

Jennifer, 18, Urban

How do I create things in my head?
I get lost somewhere quiet.
Somewhere deep inside my brain.
Far away from where I live.

Deep in a jungle of ideas.
In a place of dreams.
Somewhere only I can go.
I am the creator.

Angela, 10, Urban

SEEKING SIGNIFICANCE . . . CHARTING CHOICES

To a reasonable extent, youths become stronger by experiencing a certain amount of push-pull on their bodies, challenges to their minds, and temporary upheavals in their emotions—*stress.* These less-than-stable states enlist young people in the process of questioning the status quo and the comfort it can provide. They learn to seek answers or to create their own solutions—problem solving at its best.

Youths learn to take risks. For those involved in youth gangs, risk taking involves violence and the endangerment of themselves and others. For others, taking risks can, and often does, produce positive results. At this time in their lives, risks can involve an entire range of issues and needs.

Though young people, especially teenagers, rely on their friends for help in times of stress, they need to learn to rely on themselves more than anyone else. Adolescents must realize that many of the situations that produce psychological stress involve some level of conflict between the teenager and society itself. As long as young people give in to social demands—and peer pressures, especially those inflicted by youth gangs—they will continue to sacrifice their own identities and abilities to cope with their own lives.

Victim or Master?

Teenagers should remember that whatever happens in their lives is not the issue; how they react to situations is. *Self-awareness* can enhance how teenagers handle their stress.

I regularly work with residents of several youth institutions. My various communications classes contain teenagers who have diverse concerns and problems. As they enter the room, they inevitably "size me up" and wonder just what the program is all about, and why I think I can help them.

The first message I share is gentle, but firm. "You are not victims," I tell them. "You have the ability to control how you respond to whatever happens to you in your life."

They never fail to ask me how I know, or think I could understand, what they are going through. I explain to them that many of us are "prisoners" in our own ways. Many of us suffer from "addictions" that can hurt us: drugs, alcohol, gambling, dangerous risk taking, power. Often, we let the stress of our lives overpower us, and we succumb to our addictions.

They look at me again, and wonder what my addiction is. I tell them, "I am a recovering anorexic." I first acquired the eating disorder during my second year of law school in 1978. To feel "in control" of the grinding process of legal education, I took control of my eating and my exercise. Unfortunately, I suffered a neurological injury because of my starvation and had to quit law school five weeks before the end of my third year. For every day since then, I have dealt with the effects of its presence in my life. Every time I eat just a little too much, I fight the near-automatic impulse to purge. Stress, and a need to control my life, changed my life.

My friends helped me then, as they do now, to find within myself the ability to master my own life, one day at a time. So far, so good. So I tell the teenagers:

> Each day, find one way to create change—positive change—so that when you eventually find your way to the other side, you will not be the same person you were coming in. This changed person will be the person who is willing and able to turn negative behavior into positive thoughts and actions. It's all up to you. Your group can offer support and encouragement, and this is crucial in the process. But nobody else can rid you of the stress of change. Only you can do this. And there's no better time to start than right now.

Other teenagers can learn a message from these dialogues. Youths should accept responsibility for their own thoughts and actions. They cannot dwell on the negatives from their past that might try to pull them down. They must learn lessons—tough lessons—from their past, and they must move forward. They must reverse the idea that they might be victims and turn this attitude into a positive one. Teenagers have the ability to reduce the stress in their lives by denying a victim identity and accepting the positive identity as masters of their lives.

Villain or Hero?

Villains are people who bring out the worst in themselves and hurt others along the way. They are negative and destructive. Descriptive terms include *barbaric, brutal,* and *criminal.* Villains, contrary to the youth gang cultural beliefs, are cowards. They inflict fear, violence, and pain on others and consider this a position of strength. In fact, real strength comes from avoiding these negative behaviors. All youths—and others as well—have the potential to be villainous. Of course, this is a choice. Another choice is to act and react as a hero.

Heroes are people who have the courage to make a good thing out of their lives and the lives of others, directly or indirectly. Each young person has a hero within . . . helping to encourage self-confidence, trust, kindness, purpose, wisdom, patience, discipline, and open-mindedness. The hero within helps young people—and older people, too—understand how special they are, and that these talents can help them and others as well. The hero within encourages them to respect their bodies and their minds—whom to select as friends to nurture and support them. The hero helps them maintain honesty with themselves and others.

When young people have to make decisions about how to direct their lives, the idea of thinking about the decades beyond is unrealistic. While most children accept that they can live to be eighty or ninety years old, members of youth gangs often believe that they will die—from violence or drugs—before they are thirty.

So how can youths control whether the villain or the hero dominates their lives? I offer a few suggestions to young people.

Confront the villain within. Search within yourself and admit that you might hold negative attitudes and beliefs about yourself and life in general. Replace these negative thoughts by focusing elsewhere. List the things about your personality that get you into trouble—those things you need to change to improve your outlook. Then determine a way to change them and tackle these factors, one at a time.

Hold on tight to the hero within. Search within yourself for the positive attitudes and beliefs that you already have about yourself and everything else. Allow yourself to be proud of these positive attributes. Put them to work. Grow them.

Avoid telling yourself negative things. You talk to no one more than to yourself. Do not sabotage yourself with negative thoughts. Do not let anyone damage your positive thoughts of yourself and others.

Avoid victimhood. Feeling like a victim is easy to do and can cause long-term damage to you. It takes away your personal power and makes you vulnerable to abuse. Youth gangs prey on this sense of victimhood to get you involved in their activities.

Adopt a mentor. Other people often see in you the positive things you might not see in yourself. Mentors can give you the support you need to travel through adulthood, to achieve your goals, and to become a better person.

Keep on keepin' on. Stretch yourself, and stretch yourself some more. Learn as much as you can, and step outside your safety zone whenever you can. Youth gangs will discourage your eagerness to expand your own dreams and opportunities. Such autonomy and forward thinking threaten the cohesiveness of the gang. This alone serves to demonstrate how wonderful personal independence and growth can be for you.

FEAR

Contrary to popular belief, fear does not have to result in something negative. It can stimulate positive activity and create beneficial results. Certainly in the life of a youth gang member, the presence of fear often is the most powerful connection between that member and the gang. What would happen if, through the exploration of fear, the youth gangster learned how to put that fear to work in positive ways? To understand its broader impact and potential, let us examine the basics of fear.

From the Beginning

Most youths treat fear as a negative force. This can happen because parents and caregivers often use fear to keep their young children safe from harm. Since parents cannot always be available to protect their children, fear serves as their proxy: "Fear *every*thing, just in case *some*thing could hurt you"—crossing streets, meeting strangers, eating Halloween candy.

As children grow into adolescents, they learn to differentiate between harmful influences and safe ones. They demonstrate this especially well when they decide to do what they might fear. By *doing* what they fear, teenagers can turn fear into energy. They can learn to distinguish between activities that are truly dangerous and those that are merely fresh and untried.

Unfortunately, today as never before, a substantial portion of our youth population awakens every day in fear. This ranges from fear of family conflict to fear of outside forces, including gang violence. For many, answers to this fear remain unknown to them, at least until the community becomes involved to provide alternatives and solutions.

Worrying has played an integral part—a learned part—in human behavior since the beginning of time, according to Terry Gingras, a clinical psychologist at the Behavioral Medicine Institute. "Worry doesn't really help you with your problems. It can wear you out. You need to think instead about problem-solving." Young people need to find ways to convert their fears into energy, to expand these rushed tensions into physical energy.

For example, instead of letting their bodies tense up over an exam, teenagers can exercise for an hour as a study break the night before the test. Or, when they feel stressed about a problem with their parents, teens can take a brisk three-mile walk. They also can put that nervous energy into a karate session or writing a poem.

In addition to the fears of not being accepted, young people experience substantial fears about failure, mistakes, and—success.

Fear of Failure

Few, if any of us, like to fail, especially young people who are working each day to stabilize their identities. They do not want to fail tests, nor lose at a sporting competition, nor be dumped by their boyfriends or girlfriends.

What most teenagers do not realize, probably because they have not yet had a lot of experience, is that failure serves as a prerequisite for success. In starting the journey toward acceptance of failure as a natural learning step, one message prevails: We do not have control over all beginnings, middles, and conclusions. We do, however, have ultimate control over how we perceive and respond to this process.

Failure means different things to teenagers:

"Losing to a lesser opponent." *(Alyssa, 15, Suburban)*

"Snitching on each other." *(Dedric, 16, Inner City)*

"When you have done nothing, and don't even try to do anything." *(Kassi, 14, Rural)*

"Not getting along, excluding others, being judgmental toward each other." *(Tera, 16, Suburban)*

"Not being able to go after what we want." *(Charla, 15, Suburban)*

"Getting strung out on drugs." *(Jason, 17, Inner City)*

"Giving excuses to make up for wrongs." *(Michael, 16, Urban)*

"Making my parents ashamed of me in any way." *(Mayte, 19, Urban)*

"When a homeboy gets shot." *(Jeremy, 17, Inner City)*

Young people have viable options to help them deal with failure and to turn negatives into positives. Following are some suggestions for young people who want to master failure.

Accept that no one is perfect. Not being perfect is actually an asset. Knowing this, teenagers should remember that the only way to avoid failure is to do nothing. Where does "doing nothing" get them? Nowhere!

Avoid blaming others. By taking responsibility, youths can understand their own potential and their own limitations. They need to admit their errors and seek reasonable solutions to their problems.

Define and apply focus. Young people should determine what they want to accomplish and keep their attention on this goal until they achieve it, even if they do not reach the planned or expected end. The journey itself will help them get closer to accomplishing the next goal.

Fulfill their responsibilities. Youths learn the importance of doing their school work. When thorough, they enjoy the rewards of a job well done. The same principle applies to everything else they might consider important, from sports to social events to group commitments.

Be willing to break away from their safety zones. Young people who are willing to "take risks" create opportunities to enjoy success in new ways.

Set sights on success. When youths believe in their abilities to succeed, they have a much greater chance to experience success.

Let failure propel them forward. Life is full of failures. Rather than letting one failure lead to the next, emerging adults should let one failure provide the foundation for the next success.

Group support can enhance these suggestions for dealing with failure. Young people, particularly teenagers who are especially vulnerable to the idea of failure, should strive to surround themselves with a group of friends that reinforces the idea of success. This includes friends who trust and believe in them and their efforts to succeed. Ironically, youths who struggle with failure often have the most difficulty finding friends who focus on success. These young people are easy targets for gang recruitment. By relating to more successful peers, however, youths will have a better chance to find the stimulation to succeed.

Fear of Making Mistakes

Mistakes are related to stress and fear, because they link two important elements in the chain of learning. They connect the willingness to try with the acceptance of unplanned results. Mistakes do not necessarily translate into failure, as most perceive it. Instead of being ends in themselves, mistakes show teenagers that what they are doing needs improvement. Mistakes teach teenagers what *not* to do. Without mistakes, how would teenagers know what "next step" might be the best one?

Ordinarily, the fear of making mistakes results from *expectations*, often expectations for the unreachable accomplishment—perfection. Even when the level of desire tops at perfection, youths can hurl self-defeat on themselves by expecting themselves to:

- Do things perfectly.
- Accomplish more every single day.
- Do everything that other people expect them to do.
- Prove themselves to everyone else.
- Find satisfaction in what they do because this is what others expect of them.
- Strive for "it all" because society says so.
- Put off fun until all of the serious stuff is done.
- Weigh their own value by how other people accept them.
- Be everything to everybody.

For some unknown reason, most people consider mistakes as actions that reflect personal unworthiness, that mistakes measure weaknesses and failures. Yet, no one is perfect. In fact, imperfection prompts mistakes. Mistakes prompt better performance. And better performance prompts ultimate success.

Fear of Success

Fearing ultimate success prompts many youths not to try at all. Yes, the fear of accomplishing something perceived by others as positive often spooks young people as much as the fear of failure and the fear of making mistakes. Why?

Many young people think that success is a "rationed reward," that there is only so much to go around. If they get their share of success, then somebody else, from somewhere else, will take something very important away from them in retribution of the earlier success. Youths from inner cities are particularly affected by this rationing theory. When it is all doled out, little or none is left for them. So how can they experience that success legitimately when all the rewards are taken? Youth gangs respond to this with the appeal of profit and status generated by violence and illegal activities.

The fear of success reflects, in part, a response to the pressures that surround teenagers today. From every direction—home, school, the media, high technology, and even friends—teenagers, in particular, are reminded that "winning is everything." The pressure to succeed naturally follows this philosophy. Just as with failure, however, teenagers have their own ways to "define" success:

"Doing well in games, achieving high goals, a big 'W' in the stats." *(Alyssa, 15, Suburban)*

"Knowing that we've done our best, and always will." *(Kassi, 14, Rural)*

"Accomplishing our goals." *(Tera, 16, Suburban)*

"Appearing successful and responsible. . . . Outscoring and out-performing others." *(Karim, 17, Urban)*

"Becoming an OG, and making it without snitching, being crippled, or dying." *(Jason, 17, Inner City)*

"Completing an activity." *(Charla, 15, Suburban)*

"Being able to say I gave it my all." *(Michael, 16, Urban)*

"Getting someone back if they shoot a homeboy." *(Jeremy, 17, Inner City)*

"Being happy, never forgetting where I came from, and making my parents proud." *(Mayte, 19, Urban)*

"Moving in the direction of achieving a personal goal." *(Mallie, 18, Urban)*

"Hanging together at all times." *(Dedric, 16, Inner City)*

Definitions for success are as individual as fingerprints. Within the loose parameters of society, emerging adults must define and apply the principles of success that work for them. Why should we give teenagers so much "room" to explore? Because they will also be responsible for measuring and altering their own progress on the personal success continuum.

Rather than driving for the victory, young adults need to be reassured that their efforts—and their willingness to make mistakes—comprise the most important steps toward success that they can take. After all, no youth can be the best at everything. However, without making the effort and the mistakes, how will adults-in-training learn which choices are the best ones? This applies to scholastics, sports, socializing, family interactions, group activities, and more.

> "Right now I am confused about who I am, but feel my education is very important. However, when I see my friends from the neighborhood, they say I am "selling out" or that I am embarrassed about them. But, I am not. The people from the university tell me I need to grow up and get out of my old habits. So, my loyalties are messed up." *(Mayte, 19, Urban)*

When the group has provided a strong support system for the youth member, the group members will probably help to affirm each other and their individual thoughts, expectations, and realities.

> "What I expect from myself and others is a big consideration when I choose friends. I expect all of us to be supportive of each other in the group." *(LiAn, 16, Urban)*

> "I expect everyone, including myself, to have respect for themselves and everyone else, not just in the group. They need to be themselves and not try to be 'cool.' " *(Natalie, 17, Urban)*

TURNING TO FRIENDS

To overcome the fear of failure, making mistakes, and achieving success, young people often bypass their families and turn to their friends for support. This support can be healthy and supportive, or negative and destructive.

Friendship and Power

When teenagers turn to their friends, they often seek out *positions of influence* with those friends. For some, subtle influences include having their friends in the group listen when they speak. Nodding and agreement might provide enough reinforcement. Other youths pursue power within their group by seeking an office or a position of authority.

Still others have the potential to demonstrate aggressiveness within the group. They do not create consensus nor encourage group building. Instead, aggressors look out for themselves first, and the group second. They destroy, rather than build. Fortunately, most groups recognize the negative impact such peers have, and they "exclude" these members from participation.

Members of gangs and other antisocial groups look for different sources of friendship and power in their cliques. In the gang environment, power means "power over" someone or something else. This distorted sense of power gives the gang a channel for taking the pain, fear, or violence that its members would otherwise experience and inflicting that pain on someone else. According to Ted, a former gang member:

> We need to be more realistic about our use of the word *power*. It involves more than real uses. It involves the perception of power within a given group or gang. Many personalities "in the know" will tell us that the gangs provide a family unit, which is a big part of their recruitment strategies. This was not true for me, not the reason why my contemporaries and I joined a gang. We wanted power. We wanted the power that being in the gang brought . . . the power we felt in our guts when we walked down the street, to have citizens pull their small children and dogs indoors. We were in control. We had the power to create fear in others.

All of us start from a nonpower position: being a child. Training in power differences passes from one generation to the next by people children love and trust. Each passing includes its own level of pain, and sometimes violence. The long-term consequences of this passage can cause emotional pain or inner suffering and distress. If left unresolved, this pain will distort the child's later relationships and perceptions of the world, and his or her hopes for the future. Emotional pain might include lowered self-esteem, confusion, hopelessness, codependency, and more. It can prompt simmering anger to utter outrage, prime emotions for a gang recruit.

When the group provides the positive reinforcement that young people are seeking, the friendship will naturally follow. Power struggles usually slide into the distance, as youths seek to solidify healthy, legitimate friendships within the group.

Youth Support Groups

Friends—especially group relationships—can assert a powerful influence over one another in relieving stress and various fears. A *support group* has the ability to provide united support, assurance, and encouragement to help group members with individual decisions. A youth gang can also be a support group, however, it tends to assert its influence and pressure to frighten the member or make that youth feel weak and dependent on the gang.

Healthy youth support groups respond to this pain by providing their members with a safe place to talk about themselves—without fear—and to share feelings with friends who do not judge or test them. They especially can talk openly about how to prevent their friends from joining a youth gang.

> "Show them the results of my mistakes: the scars, the tatoos. . . . Tell them that being a gangbanger gets you locked up for a very long time." *(Tina, 17, Suburban)*

> "Tell them what it is like and how the gang treats you if they don't think you're strong enough." *(Janine, 17, Suburban)*

> "Beg and plead with him not to join." *(Douglas, 13, Inner City)*

> "Demonstrate random acts of kindness and love for that child. The wanting to belong is what she is seeking. Give it to her unconditionally." *(Marianne, 17, Urban)*

> "Make more time to spend with them so they feel they have the attention they need." *(Tonya, 17, Rural)*

> "I would talk to my friend/family member about his perceptions and discover why he really wants to join a youth gang. I would find any way I could to convince him that there are many other, healthier, more productive lifestyles than that of a gang member, no matter what the appeal." *(Olivia, 21, Urban)*

> "Tell kids about some of the consequences I have had from my own gang behavior." *(Quinton, 15, Suburban)*

"Be there for them to provide for them as they want and need to be cared for." *(Peter, 15, Urban)*

"Distract them by soaking up their time. Always call and talk with them. Stay in close contact, not only physically but emotionally as well. They need to know someone cares." *(Danna, 17, Urban)*

"I would talk to her and show her the scars from gangbanging. I would tell her stories of drive-by shootings. I would convince her that this is not what she wants to do. It will ruin her life." *(Cassandra, 15, Inner City)*

"My own experiences tell the story. My brother was a gangbanger, and he'll be in jail for the next sixty years." *(Ivory, 17, Inner City)*

"I would take a kid thinking about joining a gang to my mom and ask her how she felt when I joined a gang and served time in jail." *(Pete, 16, Inner City)*

"I would be a good listener and help my friend with his problems." *(Christopher, 18, Urban)*

"I would move my friend to another country!" *(Gary, 17, Inner City)*

"I would take her out of town, to where I was raised, and let her see what life is like in the ghetto." *(S.D., 16, Inner City)*

"Tell them how they would never get anywhere in life if they join a gang. All their dreams and hopes for a productive future will never come true if they join a gang. I would do anything and everything to save a friend." *(Dana, 16, Rural)*

"Life is too precious to sell yourself short. Gangs offer a short-term love. Real love is unconditional and doesn't hurt you or make you hurt others." *(Serena, 17, Urban)*

"Slow down and really think about what you want in life, because you are the only person who can do for yourself. None of your homies are really going to be there for you in the end." *(Louise, 17, Urban)*

"Don't join because you see—and cause—heartaches. It means a lot of fighting and killing. Gang life is a war zone." *(Joan, 16, Inner City)*

"We all get old, and we need something to fall back on. Study. Do something for yourself and don't let other people's thoughts pressure you into doing things that will lead you to a dead end, literally. Remember, if you don't care for yourself, who will?" *(Nereyda, 17, Urban)*

"No one is gonna care for you like you." *(Laquitta, 17, Urban)*

The support group offers its members the opportunity to express themselves individually. Equally important, any member of the group can candidly offer ways for another member to quit a youth gang.

"If you're gangbang, you know the outcome. This is not a game. This is real life. If you live by the gun, you're going to die by the gun. Believe that." *(Zannie, 17, Inner City)*

"I hope one day you realize what's more important to you than your gang. I hope you figure it out before you get killed." *(Andy, 17, Suburban)*

"Get out the best way you can, because gangs aren't cool. I wish somebody would have told me that when I was younger." *(C.M., 17, Inner City)*

"Get out while you can. Don't mess up your life. Don't let dollar signs catch your eye." *(Selena, 15, Suburban)*

"You don't need a gang to have high self-esteem or protection. Stand up for yourself. Protect yourself. As long as your family is behind you, nothing matters." *(Q.B., 15, Inner City)*

"Look at what you are doing to yourself and others. Take a good look at the situation from another person's perspective. You aren't acting cool. You're hurting others, especially the ones you love." *(Chanel, 16, Suburban)*

"Don't think that being in a gang is the only way to gain an identity or friendships." *(Maggie, 16, Urban)*

"Get out before you lose your life or take someone else's." *(Russ, 18, Inner City)*

"It isn't worth your freedom and family." *(Cole, 16, Inner City)*

"It's not worth dying for, or losing a family member or friend." *(Janine, 17, Suburban)*

"Move on with your life. Get out of the gang and pursue opportunities that help you be the best person you can be. Anything is possible when you free yourself from the hold of the gang. Only with this freedom can you make your real dreams come true." *(Jodi, 17, Urban)*

The youth support group provides the entire group with the opportunity to develop a cohesive relationship to work together to resolve issues. This can stimulate both individual and group empowerment.

ONE CHILD AT A TIME

From family they come—children, often ill prepared to tackle their own lives, yet too often required to rush into adulthood. School, law enforcement, church, community organizations, the media, and so many other institutions make a commitment—at some level—to help our young people along the way, to make them whole and give them purpose. That is the plan, but not all plans succeed.

In the early years, a child nurtures hopes, expectations, and dreams of the good life adults promise. Circumstances, life's realities, and unexpected happenings affect these dreams. So what makes it so different for a youth gang member? The answer is violence, crime, fear, and premature death. Yet, each gang member is still a child. In a complex world with complicated solutions, perhaps we need to return to simple thoughts.

It all comes down to one person, one child at a time. We must encourage our children to feel good about themselves, to know someone cares about them enough to listen to them and validate their worth. At the same time we must remember that "the system" is filled with red tape, long lines, and waiting lists. Yet, we must recognize, that this same system contains individuals—one person at a time—who want to save our children from lives that can destroy them and devastate those who love them.

Believing in our children as we want them to believe in themselves is a starting place. Acknowledging that dreams are universal and encouraging our children to hold their sights high and healthy is a noble undertaking. Accepting that we cannot change the world is a reality. But nurturing one child at a time is a noble challenge and a worthwhile ambition—for us all!

Chapter Highlights

- Under *stress*, young people learn to question the status quo and the comfort that it can provide. *Self-awareness* can enhance how youths handle stress.
- Youths should remember that whatever happens in their lives is not the issue; how they react to these situations is.
- *Villains* are people who bring out the worst in themselves and hurt others along the way.
- *Heroes* are people who have the courage to make something good of their lives and the lives of others, directly or indirectly.
- Most children accept that they will have long lives; most youth gang members presume that they will not live to age thirty.
- Young people can take control of the villain-versus-hero sparring within themselves. They can:

  —Confront the villain within.

  —Hold on tight to the hero within.

  —Avoid telling themselves negative things.

  —Deny personal victimhood.

  —Adopt a mentor.

  —Keep on keepin' on.

- Contrary to popular belief, fear does not have to result in something negative. However, in the life of the youth gang member, fear often serves as the most powerful connection between that member and the gang.

• Parents and caregivers often overteach children about fear to protect them from harm, real and perceived.

• Viable options to help youths deal with failure include the following:

—Accept that no one is perfect.

—Avoid blaming others.

—Define and apply focus.

—Fulfill personal responsibilities.

—Be willing to break away from safety zones.

—Set sights on success.

—Let failure propel forward movement.

• Mistakes are related to stress and fear because they link two important elements in the chain of learning. They connect the willingness to try with the acceptance of unplanned results.

• Ordinarily, the fear of making mistakes results from unrealistic expectations.

• Fearing ultimate success can prompt young people not to try at all.

• The fear of success reflects, in part, a response to the pressures that surround young people today.

• Rather than driving for the victory, young people need to be reassured that their efforts—and their willingness to make mistakes—comprise the most important steps toward success.

• In turning to their friends, teens often seek out *positions of influence* with those friends.

• In the gang environment, *power* means "power over" someone or something else.

• Friends—especially group relationships—can assert a powerful influence over one another in relieving stress and various fears.

• Healthy *support groups* have the ability to provide united support, assurance, and encouragement to help group members with individual decisions.

- Believing in our children as we want them to believe in themselves is a starting place. Accepting that we cannot change the world is a reality. Nurturing one child at a time is a noble challenge and a worthwhile ambition—for us all!

Appendix A

Organizations That Teenagers, Parents, and Those Who Work with Them Can Contact for More Information

Alliance for Children and Families
www.alliance1.org

American Youth Policy Forum
1836 Jefferson Place, NW
Washington, DC 20036–2505
Phone: 202–775–9731
Fax: 202–775–9733
www.aypf.org
aypf@aypf.org

The Association of Junior Leagues International, Inc.
660 First Avenue
New York, NY 10016–3241
Phone: 212–683–1515
Fax: 212–481–7196
www.ajli.org
info@ajli.org

Boy Scouts of America
www.bsa.scouting.org

Boys & Girls Clubs of America
1230 West Peachtree Street, NW
Atlanta, GA 30309
Phone: 404–815–5700

www.bgca.org
lmclemore@bgca.org

Campfire Boys & Girls
4601 Madison Avenue
Kansas City, MO 64112–1278
Phone: 816–756–0258
Fax: 816–756–1950
info@campfire.org

Child Welfare League of America
440 First Street, NW
Third Floor
Washington, DC 20001–2085
Phone: 202–638–2952
Fax: 202–638–4004
www.cwla.org

The Gang Crime Prevention Center
318 West Adams Street
12th Floor
Chicago, IL 60606
Phone: 888–411–4272
www.gcpc.state.il.us

Girl Scouts of the U.S.A.
member@gsusa.org

Girls Incorporated
www.girlsinc.org

JACS Volunteers
5225 Wisconsin Avenue, NW
Suite 404
Washington, DC 20015
Phone: 800–522–7773
Fax: 202–363–0239
www.jacsinc.org
sagcurrie@aol.com

National Committee to Prevent Child Abuse (NCPCA)
200 South Michigan Avenue
17th Floor

Chicago, IL 60604–4357
Phone: 312–663–3520
Fax: 312–939–8962
www.childabuse.org

National 4-H Center
7100 Connecticut Avenue
Chevy Chase, MD 20815
Phone: 301–961–2840
Phone: 1–800–368–7432
www.fourhcouncil.edu
richman@fourhcouncil.edu

National Network for Youth
www.nn4youth.org

National Urban League
120 Wall Street
New York, NY 10005
info@nul.org

National Youth Gang Center
P.O. Box 12729
Tallahassee, FL 32319
Phone: 850–385–0600
Fax: 850–386–5356
www.ncjrs.org
nygc@iir.com

Office of Juvenile Justice and Delinquency Prevention
810 Seventh Street, NW
Washington, DC 20531
Phone: 202–307–5911
http://ojjdp.ncjrs.org

Omega Boys Club
P.O. Box 884463
San Francisco, CA 94188–4463
Phone: 415–826–8664
Phone: 800-SOLDIER (765–3437)
Fax: 415–826–8673
www.street-soldiers.org
obc@street-soldiers.org

YMCA of the USA
101 North Wacker Drive
Chicago, IL 60606
Phone: 312–977–0031
Fax: 312–977–9063
www.ymca.net

Youth and Children Net
Streetcats Foundation
267 Lester Avenue
Suite 104
Oakland, CA 94606
www.child.net
youthkids@aol.com

YWCA of the USA
Empire State Building
Suite 301
350 Fifth Avenue
New York, NY 10118
Phone: 212–273–7800
Fax: 212–465–2281
www.ywca.org
jchesnutt@ywca.org

Appendix B

Survey Used by the Author in Research for This Book

In 1995, I wrote my first book about youth and family issues—*Gang Free: Friendship Choices for Today's Youth*. This book deals with how teenagers build their first friendships of choice, how they pick the groups they join, and how they resolve their basic social needs during adolescence. It is a comprehensive look at the issues of adolescence from the perspective of teens and their families. Because of *Gang Free*, I moved to the issue of gangs and continue to work with media and community organizations throughout the United States and Canada to help resolve gang-related issues.

In 1997, while I was serving my first session as a Nevada state senator, Greenwood Publishing Group approached me to write a book for school and public libraries. They asked for a book that would focus on how to keep youth from joining gangs and how to help disengage those who have already joined. I said "yes." I read four dozen books on the issue and did other extensive research. Now it is time for me to get input from the kids themselves—to include YOUR ideas, concerns, and suggestions. This is why I need YOUR assistance with *Winning the War Against Youth Gangs: A Guide for Teens, Families, and Communities*.

Would you please help me by completing the following survey. Your answers will enhance the material in my book. More so, your input will influence the readers—teenagers, families, and educators. When your quotes are used, I will give you full credit by using only your first name, age, and where you live, as you describe below (e.g., inner city). Your answers will also be included in statistical analyses of the subject.

In advance, thank you for your kind assistance. The information you provide will be invaluable to those who read the book.

Valerie Wiener

* * * * *

Your name _____ Age _____

Complete address _____

_____

Which best describes where you live? Please check one:
_____ urban _____ rural _____ inner city _____suburban

Please sign ONLY ONE of the following releases:

YES. I authorize the author to include my name/age/area where I live when she uses my input for quotes. Please sign to give the author your permission.

_____

YES. I authorize the author to use my quote(s) with my age and where I live, but I prefer that she identify me by a different name. Please sign if this is your preference. _____

NO. I do not want the author to use my quotes or name, but she can use my input to help with statistical analyses. Please sign if this is your preference.

_____

1. In 25 words or less, what does *friendship* mean to you? _____

_____

_____

2. Which "needs" do you look to your group to satisfy for you? (Check all that apply)
_____ Belonging
_____ Opportunities, rewards
_____ Peer approval
_____ Family replacement
_____ Refuge, safety, privacy
_____ Status, identity
_____ Shared time, space, activity, interest
_____ Other (please explain) _____

_____

3. How did you get associated with your current group of friends? (Check ALL that apply)

_____ I was recruited

_____ My friends were already involved

_____ My family was already involved

_____ Peer pressure

_____ I had few, if any, other choices

_____ I knew it was the best group for my needs

_____ My family encouraged me to join

_____ I felt comfortable with the other group members

_____ Other (please explain) _____

_____

4. How much influence do your parents or family exercise over your choice of friends?   _____ Very much   _____ Some   _____ Very little   _____ None

5. How would you define a *youth gang*? _____

_____

_____

6. Have you ever been approached to join a youth gang? _____ Yes   _____ No

If yes, at what age were you first approached to join? _____

If you joined, at what age did you join? _____

7. What was your reason for joining or NOT joining the gang? _____

_____

_____

_____

_____

8. If you could, would you keep your best friend or family member from joining a youth gang?

_____ Yes   _____ No   Why? _____

_____

_____

_____

9. If yes to #8, what would YOU do to prevent this from happening? _____

_____

_____

_____

10. How can/should the following groups help PREVENT KIDS FROM JOINING youth gangs?

Families _____

_____

Schools _____

_____

Law enforcement _____

_____

Community organizations _____

_____

Churches _____

_____

Government _____

_____

Businesses _____

_____

Media _____

_____

Other (please specify) _____

_____

11. If your best friend or a family member were in a youth gang, what positive and legal steps would you take to help get that person out of the gang? _____

_____

_____

12. How can/should the following groups help REMOVE kids from the gangs they have joined?

Families _____

_____

Schools _____

_____

Law enforcement _____

_____

Community organizations _____

_____

Churches _____

_____

Government _____

_____

Businesses _____

Media _____

Other (please specify) _____

13. How do you feel about the use of violence as a way of:
Getting and keeping power over others? _____

Resolving your own conflicts? _____

Protecting yourself and others? _____

Other reasons/uses (please describe) _____

14. Please check under the appropriate description the importance—to you—
of the following:

	Top Priority	Very Important	Important	Moderately Important	Insignificant
Education					
Current or future job opportunities					
Safe/secure neighborhood					
Family					
Friends					
Financial wealth					
Power					
Status					
Personal safety					

15. How would you describe the influence of youth gangs in your community? (Check ALL that apply) ____ Ever-present ____ Fear-provoking
____ Insignificant ____ Destructive ____ More hype than reality
____ Positive ____ Threatening ____ Unifying ____ Protective
____ Other (explain) _____

16. If you were to describe a "typical" youth gang member to a stranger, what would you say? _____

_____

_____

_____

17. If you had one piece of advice to give to a youth gang member, what would that be? _____

_____

_____

_____

18. Please feel free to share any additional comments about the book and/or its subject matter _____

_____

_____

_____

Please return this questionnaire to:
Valerie Wiener
Wiener Communications Group
1500 Foremaster Lane
Las Vegas, NV 89101
Fax: (702) 221-9239 * E-mail: VWiener@aol.com

Thank you so much for your invaluable assistance!

Bibliography

Atkin, Beth S. *Voices from the Streets: Young Former Gang Members Tell Their Stories.* Boston: Little, Brown, and Company, 1996.

Branden, Nathaniel. *The Power of Self-Esteem.* Deerfield Beach, Fla.: Health Communications, 1992.

Cervantes, Richard C., ed. *Substance Abuse and Gang Violence.* Newbury Park, Calif.: Sage Publications, 1992.

Chaiken, Marcia R. *Kids, COPS, and Communities.* Washington, D.C.: U.S. Department of Justice/National Institute of Justice, 1998.

Cohen, Albert K. *Delinquent Boys: The Culture of the Gang.* New York: The Free Press, 1955.

Creighton, Allan, and Paul Kivel. *Helping Teens Stop Violence: A Practical Guide for Counselors, Educators, and Parents.* Alameda, Calif.: Hunter House, 1992.

Cunegine, Hattie. *Choices for Teenagers.* Ann Arbor, Mich.: Proctor Publications, 1996.

Davis, Douglas. *The Five Myths of Television Power.* New York: Simon & Schuster, 1993.

Decker, Scott H., and Barrik Van Winkle. *Life in the Gang: Family, Friends, and Violence.* Oakleigh, Melbourne, Australia: Cambridge University Press, 1996.

Dinkmeyer, Don. *Raising a Responsible Child.* New York: Fireside, 1973.

Fleming, Don, and Laurel J. Schmidt. *How to Stop the Battle with Your Teenager.* New York: Fireside, 1989.

Gockley, Gil, and Tanya Tihansky Gockley. *Loving Is Natural; Parenting Is Not: Creating a Value-Centered Family.* Rochester, N.Y.: Coleman Press, 1997.

Goldstein, Arnold P., and C. Ronald Huff, eds. *The Gang Intervention Handbook.* Champaign, Ill.: Research Press, 1993.

Greenberg, Keith Elliot. *Out of the Gang.* Minneapolis, Minn.: Lerner Publications, 1992.

Howell, James C. *Risk Factors for Gang Membership, Ages 10 to 12.* Presentation to the Nevada State Legislature Interim Study on Juvenile Justice (from a study by Hill, Howell, Hawkins, and Battin), 1998.

Jamieson, Kathleen Hall, and Karlyn Kohrs Campbell. *The Interplay of Influence: News Advertising, Politics, and the Mass Media.* Belmont, Calif.: Wadsworth Publishing Company, 1992.

Jones, Barbara Barrington, and Brad Wilcox. *What Teenagers Wish They Could Tell You.* Salt Lake City, Utah: Deseret Book Company, 1994.

Kelling, George L., and Catherine M. Coles. *Fixing Broken Windows.* New York: Touchstone, 1996.

Kirshanbaum, Mira. *Parent/Teen Breakthrough.* New York: Plume, 1991.

Kissane, Sharon F. *Gang Awareness: What You Can Do.* Kettering, Ohio: PPI Publishing, 1995.

Klein, Malcolm. *The American Street Gang: Its Nature, Prevalence, and Control.* New York: Oxford University Press, 1995.

Klein, Malcolm W., Cheryl L. Maxson, and Jody Miller. *The Modern Gang Reader.* Los Angeles: Roxbury Publishing Company, 1995.

Korem, Dan. *Suburban Gangs: The Affluent Rebels.* Richardson, Tex.: International Focus Press, 1994.

Lal, Shirley R., Dhyan Lal, and Charles M. Achilles. *Handbook on Gangs in Schools: Strategies to Reduce Gang-Related Activities.* Newbury Park, Calif.: Corwin Press, 1993.

Lazere, Donald, ed. *American Media and Mass Culture.* Berkeley: University of California Press, 1987.

McIntire, Roger W. *Teenagers and Parents: Ten Steps for a Better Relationship.* Columbia, Md.: Summit Crossroads Press, 1996.

Maté, Ferenc. *A Reasonable Life.* N.p.: Alabatros Publishing, 1993.

Mayer, Martin. *Making News.* Boston: Harvard Business School Press, 1993.

Medved, Michael. *Hollywood Versus America.* New York: HarperPerennial, 1992.

Milionis, Steve. *Dealing with Adolescent Conflict: A Parent's Practical Guide to Effective Communication Skills.* Hayden Lake, Idaho: Milionis Education Consulting Firm, 1996.

Muehlbauer, Gene, and Laura Dodder. *The Losers: Gang Delinquency in an American Suburb.* Westport, Conn.: Praeger, 1983.

Mulroy, Darrell, and Dinah Tallent. *No Cuffs: Police Issues Teenagers Face.* Kettering, Ohio: PPI Publishing, 1995.

Myers, Bob. *Parenting Teenagers in the 1990s.* Hawthorn, Victoria, Australia: ACER, Ltd., 1992.

Myers, Bob. *Raising Responsible Teenagers.* London: Jessica Kingsley Publishers, 1996.

On Alert! Gang Prevention: School In-Service Guidelines. Sacramento, Calif.: California Department of Education, 1994.

Padilla, Felix M. *The Gang as an American Enterprise.* New Brunswick, N.J.: Rutgers University Press, 1996.

Rushkoff, Douglas. *Media Virus.* New York: Ballantine Books, 1994.

Sachs, Steven L. *Street Gang Awareness: A Resource Guide for Parents and Professionals.* Minneapolis, Minn.: Fairview Press, 1997.

Safe Schools Manual: A Resource on Making Schools, Communities, and Families Safe for Our Children. Washington, D.C.: National Education Association, 1996.

Sikes, Gini. *8 Ball Chicks.* New York: Anchor Books, 1997.

Spergel, Irving A. *The Youth Gang Problem: A Community Approach.* New York: Oxford University Press, 1995.

Taylor-Gerdes, Elizabeth. *Straight Up!* Chicago: Lindsey Publishing, 1996.

Trapani, Margi. *Working Together Against Gang Violence.* New York: The Rosen Publishing Group, 1996.

Urban Street Gang Enforcement. Washington, D.C.: Bureau of Justice Assistance, 1997.

Weeks, Robin, and Cathy Spatz Widom. *Early Childhood Victimization Among Incarcerated Adult Male Felons.* Washington, D.C.: National Institute of Justice, 1998.

Wiener, Valerie. *Gang Free: Friendship Choices for Today's Youth.* Minneapolis, Minn.: Fairview Press, 1995.

Wiener, Valerie. *The Nesting Syndrome: Grown Children Living at Home.* Minneapolis, Minn.: Fairview Press, 1997.

Williams, Stanley. *Gangs and Your Friends.* Center City, Minn.: Hazelden, 1997.

Wilson, John J., and James C. Howell. *Serious, Violent, and Chronic Juvenile Offenders: A Comprehensive Strategy.* Washington, D.C.: Office of Juvenile Justice and Delinquency Prevention, 1993.

Zuba, Marge Tye. *"Wish I Could've Told You": Portraits of Teenagers Almost Dropping Out.* DeKalb, Ill.: LEPS Press/Northern Illinois University, 1995.

Index

tencing and sentencing alternatives in, 110–11
Juvenile delinquency, 35, 73

Kirshanbaum, Mira, 4
Kissane, Sharon F., 126
Korem, Dan, 50, 96

Language, and group identity, 24–25
Law enforcement: communication and counseling skills of, 107–9; gang-control measures, 106; gang-suppression measures, 92–93, 103–5; mandates for, 104; saturation-policing, 105; school-based, 118
Life in the Gang, 76, 164
Loners, 49; teenagers as, 27

Maté, Ferenc, 131
Materialism: and gang-related crime, 70, 71–73; and media influence, 140–41
Media, 129–41; and community alliances, 145; cultural impact of, 131–33; and dysfunctional families, 132; and entertainment programming, 133–35; and materialism, 140–41; news, influence and methodology of, 135–38; potential/ideal uses of, 138–39; responsibility of, 133–39; viewer control of, 139–40; violence, 44, 139. *See also* Television
Medved, Michael, 139
Mentoring, 150, 178
Merging, 23
Misbehavior: and discipline, 161–62; and gang membership, 51–52; motivations for, 35–37
Missing Protector Factor, 61
Mules, 72–73
Multigroup membership, 27
Music, and group identity, 24
Myers, Bob, 35

National youth service, 146–47
Neighborhood, at-risk, 52–53
Neighborhood organizations, 151–52
Nesting Syndrome, The, 131

Occultic gangs, 50
Office of Juvenile Justice and Delinquency Prevention (OJJDP), 93, 150
Original gangsters (OGs), 53
Outreach services, 90
Outsiders, 27; gang members as, 99

Parent/Teen Breakthrough, 4
Parental involvement, levels of, 165–66
Parental networks, 169
Parenting Teenagers in the 1990s, 35–36
Parents/parenting, 126; absent, 34; authority of, 159–61; and children's needs, 10–11; combative style of, 33; and discipline, 161–62; friendly style of, 33; and gang disengagement participation, 165–66; gang prevention strategies for, 94, 167–71; outrageous behavior of, 33–34; over-critical, 33; and power and control issues, 31–32, 36–37; and praise and reward, 162–64; responsible, 34; as role models, 4, 8, 167; roles, 159–64; and school-based interventions, 124; and setting of limits and rules, 159–60; styles, 32–34
Peer approval, 20–21
Peer conflict, resolution of, 37–40, 120–21
Peer groups, 13–28; defined, 18; exclusion from and refusal to join, 27; friendship rights in, 19–20; versus gangs, 45; merging process in, 23–28; and multigroup membership, 27; and shared interests, 25–26; as support system, 184. *See also* Friendship
Peer mediation programs, 120–21

About the Author

VALERIE WIENER is a state senator from Nevada. She has been actively involved with youth issues and youth communications projects since the early 1970s and is the author of *Gang Free: Friendship Choices for Today's Youth* (1995).